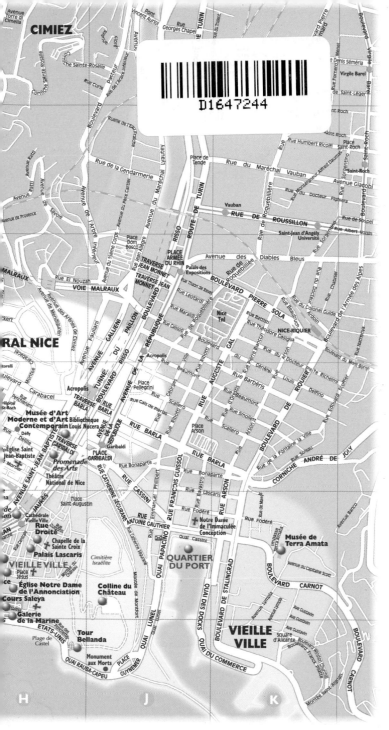

# CITYPACK TOP 25
# Nice

**DONNA DAILEY**

If you have any comments
or suggestions for this guide
you can contact the editor at
*Citypack@theAA.com*

**AA Publishing**
Find out more about AA Publishing and the wide
range of services the AA provides by visiting our
website at www.theAA.com/travel

# How to Use This Book

## KEY TO SYMBOLS

✚ Map reference to the accompanying fold-out map

⊠ Address

☎ Telephone number

⊙ Opening/closing times

🍴 Restaurant or café

🚆 Nearest rail station

🚍 Nearest bus route

⛴ Nearest riverboat or ferry stop

♿ Facilities for visitors with disabilities

❷ Other practical information

▷ Further information

ℹ Tourist information

✋ Admission charges: Expensive (over €8), Moderate (€4–€8) and Inexpensive (€4 or less)

👣 Major Sight   ★ Minor Sight

👣👣 Walks   🚌 Excursions

🎟 Shops

🎵 Entertainment and Nightlife

🍽 Restaurants

### This guide is divided into four sections

• **Essential Nice:** An introduction to the city and tips on making the most of your stay.
• **Nice by Area:** We've broken the city into five areas, and recommended the best sights, shops, entertainment venues, nightlife and restaurants in each one. Suggested walks help you to explore on foot.
• **Where to Stay:** The best hotels, whether you're looking for luxury, budget or something in between.
• **Need to Know:** The info you need to make your trip run smoothly, including getting about by public transport, weather tips, emergency phone numbers and useful websites.

**Navigation** In the Nice by Area chapter, we've given each area its own colour, which is also used on the locator maps throughout the book and the map on the inside front cover.

**Maps** The fold-out map accompanying this book is a comprehensive street plan of Nice. The grid on this fold-out map is the same as the grid on the locator maps within the book. We've given grid references within the book for each sight and listing.

# Contents

CONTENTS

3

# Introducing Nice

She's the Queen of the Riviera and proudly flaunts her jewels: emerald gardens, sapphire sea, a gold and ruby-hued old town and belle-époque gems strung along her seaside necklace, the Promenade des Anglais. Discover Nice in all her glory.

One in every hundred visitors to Europe spends at least one night in Nice. For some, this beautiful city curving around the Baie des Anges (Bay of Angels) is the gateway to the glamorous resorts of the Côte d'Azur. For many, it's a heavenly destination in itself, full of fine art, lovely architecture, good restaurants and chic shopping. Visitors can slip easily into the *dolce vita* of this vibrant Mediterranean city.

Nice's wonderful location gives the city much of its beauty and character. Its entire southern boundary is the sea, with wooded hills on either side. The foothills of the Maritime Alps form its northern backdrop, their peaks rising to over 2,740m (9,000ft) only 50km (31 miles) from the coast. To the east, the Italian border lies less than 30km (19 miles) away.

Nice only became part of France in 1860. For nearly 500 years prior, it was largely ruled by the Counts of Savoy and was part of the Kingdom of Sardinia. This mixed heritage is evident in its architecture and traditions, but Nice isn't just a French city with Italian accents. It has a strong, separate identity, with its own language (*Nissart*), cuisine, AOCs for olive oil and wine—and its own style.

The legacy of the great artists who found inspiration on the Riviera lives on in the city's trendy art galleries and boutiques. The old town, no longer a dodgy area, is now the nightlife spot for local people and visitors alike. And while there is an upmarket air to parts of the city, the whole town lets its hair down during the Nice Carnival. Then, and during the glorious summer, all of Nice takes to the streets. Join them!

# Facts + Figures

**Size:** 5th-largest city in France
**Population:** 380,000 (half under 40)
**Coastline:** 10km (6 miles)
**Beaches:** 7.5km (4.5 miles)
**Parks/gardens:** 300ha (740 acres)
**Classified historical monuments:** 32
**Ponds and fountains:** 150

## BOOM TOWN

Every day at noon a cannon is fired from the top of the Colline du Château, the hill between the Vieille Ville and quai du Port, startling visitors in the old town down below. The story goes that a retired English colonel from India started the custom to remind his young wife, who was always late, that it was time to come home and cook him his lunch.

4

## SECOND CITY

After Paris, Nice is the top tourist destination in France. It has the busiest airport outside the capital, serving nearly 10 million passengers each year, 57 per cent of whom come from abroad; some 20 budget airlines also make it the top French airport for low-cost flights. Nice has the most hotel facilities and the most municipal museums and galleries of any city in France other than Paris. It is the country's leading convention city after Paris—the Acropolis has been voted the best European Convention Centre several times.

## MUNICIPAL BARGAINS

Nice's municipal museums are free on the first and third Sundays of each month, and every day for visitors with disabilities and those under 18. A seven-day museum pass allows entry to every municipal museum (excluding the Chagall and Asian Arts museums) for €6.

# A Short Stay in Nice

**DAY 1**

**Morning** Start at the west end of **Cours Saleya** (▷ 26–27) and walk through the flower market. Bear right at the end of place Charles Félix and continue along rue des Ponchettes to the *ascenceur* (lift) for the **Colline du Château** (▷ 25) at Tour Bellanda. Go up and admire the views over the old town and coast, and the port on the opposite side.

**Mid-morning** Return to place Charles Félix. Have a coffee at one of the cafés and enjoy people-watching in the square. Then stroll north along rue Jules Gilly and rue Droite through the **Vieille Ville** (▷ 30–31).

**Lunch** From place St-François, continue north on rue Pairolière to **Chez René Socca** (▷ 39) and join the queue for a portion of *socca*, one of Nice's favourite treats.

**Afternoon** The striking **Musée d'Art Moderne et d'Art Contemporain** (▷ 60–61) is just ahead beyond place Garibaldi. Spend a couple of hours here perusing the collection and the sculptures on the esplanade. You'll see all the main avant-garde movements from the 1960s onwards. Then walk down the **Promenade du Paillon** (▷ 62) to the seafront.

**Dinner** Walk east along the Promenade des Anglais, which becomes the quai des Etats-Unis opposite the Vieille Ville. Cross the road and walk through the arcades into Cours Saleya and the old town. Have dinner at **Restaurant du Gésu** (▷ 40) or **La Feniera** (▷ 39) for authentic, inexpensive *Cuisine Nissarde*, such as *boeuf en daube à la Niçoise* or home-made gnocchi.

**Evening** Stop off at **Wayne's** (▷ 38) or one of the other bars along rue de la Préfecture for a nightcap and some live music.

## DAY 2

**Morning** The double-decker tour bus, **Nice Le Grand Tour** (▷ 119), is an excellent way to get an overview of the city. Get an early start and pick up a picnic lunch on your way to the Promenade des Anglais. The first bus departs at 9.30 (check times locally) from its stop on the seaward side of the promenade, opposite the carousel in Jardin Albert I. Halfway through the tour, get off at stop 7. From here you can visit the **Musée Henri Matisse** (▷ 72–73) and the **Parc des Arènes de Cimiez** (▷ 76–77).

**Lunch** Walk through the Parc des Arènes to the **Monastère Franciscain de Cimiez** (▷ 78). Have your picnic lunch in the monastery gardens.

**Afternoon** Catch the next Nice Le Grand Tour bus downhill to the next stop to visit the **Musée Marc Chagall** (▷ 74–75). Then return to the bus and finish the tour, which ends back on the Promenade des Anglais.

**Mid-afternoon** Walk west along the promenade to the **Hôtel Negresco** (▷ 44–45). Treat yourself to afternoon tea at **Brasserie La Rotonde** (▷ 54). Walk it off with a longer stroll on the promenade, or some shopping in the designer stores along rue Paradis.

**Dinner** Walk along avenue de Verdun to **Place Masséna** (▷ 59), with its stunning Fontaine du Soleil (Fountain of the Sun). Just down the steps on rue de l'Opéra is **Lou Nissart** (▷ 68), which serves delicious fish soup and other *Nissarde* specialities.

**Evening** Stroll into the old town to place Rossetti for an ice cream at **Fenocchio** (▷ 39). Enjoy the lively atmosphere and the lovely view of the cathedral lit at night.

# Top 25

## ►►►

**Antibes ▷ 82–83**
Massive coastal ramparts lead to Europe's largest yacht harbour.

**Cagnes-sur-Mer ▷ 86**
Renoir's house is in an olive grove below this peaceful medieval village.

**Cannes ▷ 84–85**
Glamorous resort and home of the famous Film Festival.

**Villefranche-sur-Mer ▷ 94** Explore the steep streets behind the brightly painted waterfront houses.

**Villa Ephrussi de Rothschild ▷ 93**
Palatial pink villa with enchanting gardens and musical fountains.

**Vieille Ville ▷ 30–31**
Find the life and soul of Nice here in the old town.

**Quartier du Port ▷ 29**
Pretty Italian façades line the picturesque port.

**Promenade des Anglais ▷ 48–49** Stroll along this palm-lined, seaside promenade.

**Place Masséna ▷ 59** Huge, handsome pedestrian square at the start of the new town.

**Parc des Arènes de Cimiez ▷ 76–77**
Roman ruins and an archaeological museum.

**Palais Lascaris ▷ 28**
Baroque decor and musical instruments in an exquisite old-town mansion.

**Musée Marc Chagall ▷ 74–75** Monumental paintings and stained glass with a Biblical theme.

Map labels: Fondation Maeght, Grasse · Cathédrale Orthodoxe Russe · PROMENADE DES ANGLAIS 41–54 · Musée des Beaux-Arts · Hôtel Negresco · Promenade des Anglais · Antibes, Cagnes-sur-Mer, Cannes

These pages are a quick guide to the Top 25, which are described in more detail later. Here they are listed alphabetically, and the tinted background shows which area they are in.

**Cathédrale Orthodoxe Russe** ▷ **58** Beautiful onion-domed jewel, built by Russian expatriates.

**Cathédrale Sainte-Réparate** ▷ **24** An old town landmark dedicated to Nice's patron saint.

**Colline du Château** ▷ **25** Catch the breeze and enjoy the views at this delightful hilltop park.

**Cours Saleya** ▷ **26–27** The lively site of Nice's famous flower market.

**Èze** ▷ **87** Stunning panoramic views of the Côte d'Azur from atop this medieval village.

**Fondation Maeght** ▷ **88** A world-class art museum set among the pines in St-Paul-de-Vence.

**Grasse** ▷ **89** This town is the perfume capital of the world.

**Hôtel Negresco** ▷ **44–45** Belle-époque jewel on the Promenade des Anglais.

**Monaco-Ville** ▷ **90–91** The old fortified town of the principality of Monaco.

**Monte-Carlo** ▷ **92** Its glittering casino is the home of the high rollers.

*Map labels:*
- **CIMIEZ 69–78**
- Parc des Arènes de Cimiez
- Musée Henri Matisse
- Le Paillon Tort
- Musée Marc Chagall
- **CENTRAL NICE 55–68**
- Musée d'Art Moderne et d'Art Contemporain
- Promenade des Arts
- Promenade du Paillon
- Cathédrale Sainte-Réparate
- Palais Lascaris
- **VIEILLE VILLE 20–40**
- Cimitière Israélite
- Place Masséna
- VIEILLE VILLE
- QUARTIER DU PORT
- Jardin Albert I
- Cours Saleya
- Colline du Château
- Èze, Monaco-Ville, Monte-Carlo, Villa Ephrussi de Rothschild, Villefranche-sur-Mer

**Musée Henri Matisse** ▷ **72–73** A fascinating collection of artworks and personal belongings.

**Musée des Beaux-Arts** ▷ **46–47** An important fine arts collection housed in a beautiful mansion.

**Musée d'Art Moderne et d'Art Contemporain** ▷ **60–61** Modern art from the 1960s onwards.

# Shopping

You should find everything you're looking for on a shopping spree in Nice, whether you want chic designer outfits, trendy chain-store fashions, department-store bargains, fine art, handmade crafts, hip home decor, priceless antiques, flea-market finds, gourmet goodies or a whole lot of bright-coloured, sweet-smelling Provençal products. Shopping is especially fun when you take in some of the wonderful markets, which sell everything from food to flowers.

### Designer Fashions and Fine Food

From sportswear to evening wear, most of the top names in French fashion are represented in Nice. The smartest shops are in a tiny triangle between Place Masséna and the Promenade des Anglais, along rue Paradis, avenue de Verdun and avenue de Suède. Here you'll find Kenzo, Armani, Sonia Rykiel, Lacoste and others. Even if your purse only stretches to window-shopping here, the displays are inspiring. You'll find even more designer names and luxury shops in Cannes, as every brand wants a presence in this glamorous city. If that Cartier watch is beyond your budget, buy a taste of luxury at LeNotre (▷ 102) and Cavier House. Cannes has the only branches outside Paris.

### Regional Produce

The region produces so many wonderful local products that you'll wish you'd brought another suitcase. The olive oil is particularly superior—Nice has its own AOC label of quality—while tapenades, olive pastes and the like are easy to

---

**FRENCH FLAIR**

The French bring a certain flair to everyday living, and Nice is a good place to shop for stylish practical items that you're unlikely to see at home. Even simple notebooks and stationery are attractively presented. Look for high-quality cookware and useful kitchen gadgets. Home decor shops are popular in Nice, featuring trendy but tasteful furniture, accessories and soft furnishings.

*Shopping choices range from vibrant blooms in the flower market to Provençal wine, soap or fashion*

take home. Another specialty is crystallized fruits and flower petals, and these sugary delicacies are well worth trying. The best are from Confiserie Florian (▷ 36). The hard, oblong biscuits called *navettes* are a Provençal tradition and are delicious flavoured with lavender, orange and other scents. Look, too, for lemon products from Menton. Local cheeses, honey, spices, jams and wines are other edible options.

## Scents and Colours

The abundance of flowers and fruits in the Provençal countryside made Grasse the heart of perfume-making. A perfume or scented soap from one of the top perfume factories will ensure lingering memories of your visit. Several have workshops where you can create your own signature perfume. Table linens, children's dresses, baskets, pottery and souvenirs in bright Provençal hues are inexpensive and useful gifts that look good back home.

## Arts and Crafts

There's no more appropriate purchase than a painting, sculpture or drawing in this land that inspired so many great artists. There are art galleries throughout Nice's old town and up and down the Côte d'Azur, where you'll find artworks to suit every taste and budget. Some towns are renowned for their ceramics or glass-making, and the workshops are fun places to browse and buy. There are also many craft markets where you can find unusual gifts.

### WHAT'S WHERE

As well as in a dedicated district near the port, antiques markets are held regularly in Nice's Cours Saleya and elsewhere. Galeries Lafayette is Nice's leading department store, while FNAC and Virgin are the places for music, books and media. Look for cheeses in *fromageries*, bread and baguettes in *boulangeries*, pastries and cakes in *pâtisseries*, cold meats in *charcuteries*, confectionery in *confiseries*. *Bouquinistes* sell used books and prints, *tabacs* sell tobacco and other items.

# Shopping by Theme

The shops in and around Nice have everything from vibrant Provençal ceramics to designer fashions, from olive oil to chic kitchenware. On this page we list shops by theme. For a more detailed write-up of each one, see Nice by Area.

## ACCESSORIES

Hermès (▷ 64)
Louis Vuitton (▷ 52)

## ANTIQUES

Village Ségurane (▷ 37)

## ART AND CRAFTS

Art-DAC (▷ 36)
Le Bazar de l'Hôtel de Ville (▷ 101)
Centre d'Art Haitien (▷ 36)
Le Chandelier (▷ 36)
Diagram (▷ 36)
Etnosud (▷ 37)
Galerie Le Capricorne (▷ 102)
Galerie Farinelli (▷ 101)
Galerie Madoura (▷ 102)
Lalique (▷ 102)
Transparence (▷ 37)
Verrerie de Biot (▷ 101)

## BOOKS

Heidi's English Bookshop (▷ 101)

## CHILDREN'S GIFTS

Enfant ti Age (▷ 64)

## FASHION

Anne Fontaine (▷ 52)
Boutique Lacoste (▷ 52)
Claude Bonucci (▷ 52)
DMC (▷ 101)
The Earth Collection (▷ 37)
Eden Gray (▷ 101)
Emporio Armani (▷ 52)
Espace Harroch (▷ 52)
Façonnable (▷ 52)
Jacques Loup (▷ 102)
Max Mara (▷ 64)
Sonia Rykiel (▷ 52)

## FLOWERS

Marché aux Fleurs (▷ 37)

## FOOD AND DRINK

À l'Olivier (▷ 36)
Balade en Provence (▷ 36, 101)
Cave Caprioglio (▷ 36)
Confiserie Florian (▷ 36)
La Cure Gourmande (▷ 36)
L'Empereur (▷ 101)
Ets Vallauri (▷ 102)
La Ferme Fromagère (▷ 64)
Fromagerie Ceneri (▷ 101)
LeNôtre (▷ 102)
Lou Canice (▷ 37)
Moulin à Huile Alziari (▷ 37)
Oliviera (▷ 37)
Terre des Truffes (▷ 37)

## GIFTS

Hôtel Negresco gift shops (▷ 52)
Le Papier (▷ 64)
Saint-Paul Images (▷ 102)

## HATS

Lilô Chapô (▷ 102)

## HOME

Augustin Latour (▷ 52)
Au Tombeau de la Vaisselle (▷ 36)
Créanova (▷ 64)
Kitchen Bazaar (▷ 64)
Loft Design (▷ 64)

## JEWELLERY

Cartier (▷ 64)
Clair Obscur (▷ 36)
Elizabeth Contal (▷ 64)
Les Néréïdes (▷ 52)

## PERFUME

Chanel (▷ 52)
Fragonard (▷ 102)
Galimard (▷ 102)
Molinard (▷ 37, 102)

## SHOPPING MALL

Nice Étoile (▷ 64)

# Nice by Night

For most visitors, Nice at night is a low-key affair, involving a stroll along the Promenade des Anglais or through the old town. But life at a faster pace is there if you want it, with casinos open until dawn and a club scene, too. Nice loves its music, and summer in the city brings various musical events and festivals, many involving free concerts.

### After-dark Atmosphere

The old town is the hub of Nice's nightlife. As the sun goes down, the bars fill up along Cours Saleya and rue de la Préfecture. Many along rue de la Préfecture have live music, making it a particularly animated stretch. Nearby, local young people gather on the steps of the Palais de Justice to plan their night out. For after-dark atmosphere, head for place Rossetti, where the spotlit cathedral casts a warm glow over the lively square. Or stroll along the Promenade des Anglais. In central Nice, the pedestrian streets fanning out from place Magenta are also popular spots for an early-evening drink, watching the buskers and mime artists.

### Entertainment Options

You can find just about any kind of entertainment you want in Nice, from Irish pubs to luxury bars, smoky jazz cafés, hot Latin clubs, live rock and soul music or disco beats. Free concerts are often held in Place Masséna, so watch for local adverts or ask around when the stage and lighting equipment goes up. Nice has two casinos, and there are many more up and down the Côte d'Azur.

*Try your luck at the casino, enjoy a relaxed meal in Cours Saleya or take a seafront stroll*

---

**BEYOND NICE**

It's only 45 minutes from Nice to Cannes by train, and less than 30 minutes to Monte-Carlo, making most of the Côte d'Azur your playground for an evening out. You can roll the dice in style at the Monte-Carlo Casino (▷ 92), go to Cannes for the Fireworks Festival nights (▷ 104) or try the Antibes and Juan-les-Pins Jazz Festival (▷ panel, 104).

# Eating Out

Dining out is one of the great pleasures of Nice, whether it be at a Michelin-starred restaurant, an atmospheric place in the old town or a simple snack, such as *socca*.

### Budget Choices
Even if you're on a budget you can eat well in Nice. Many restaurants in the old town and city centre have three-course evening menus of simple but delicious local dishes for €12–€20, with wine by the carafe at €8–€15. Pasta and pizza are on most menus. Many ethnic restaurants, especially from North Africa, Turkey and even Afghanistan, are also good value.

### Be Sure to Try
Among the many dishes to try are gnocchi, which was invented in Nice, not Italy; *boeuf en daube* (beef cooked in a savoury sauce with red wine, onions and herbs), *mesclun* (a salad of mixed greens gathered on the hills), *farci* (stuffed vegetables), *beignets* (vegetables deep-fried in batter), courgette flowers (batter-fried, a local favourite), and, of course, *salade niçoise*, with tuna, egg, anchovies, olives and vegetables.

### Helpful Hints
You can dress casually in all but the top restaurants. Service is usually included (*service compris*) so you don't need to tip unless you wish to. For a few euros, takeaways like *socca* (▷ panel, 39) and *pissaladière* (▷ panel, 40) can make a quick and tasty alternative to a sit-down lunch. Nice shares with Italy a love of ice cream. The old town in particular is packed with ice-cream parlours.

---

**OPENING TIMES**

Most restaurants open for lunch at noon and serve until around 2.30. They reopen at around 7 or 7.30 for dinner and take orders until around 10. Many stay open later in summer. Brasseries and cafés stay open throughout the day and often remain open later at night than restaurants, sometimes until 1am in busy tourist areas.

*Ready for lunch; a drink by the sea; biscuits from La Cure Gourmande; tables set at Le Louis XV*

# Restaurants by Cuisine

Although the restaurants in Nice are predominantly French and/or Niçois/Provençal, there is also a strong international influence. Here restaurants are listed by cuisine. For more detailed descriptions see Nice by Area.

## AFGHAN

Restaurant Pamir (▷ 40)

## BISTRO/BRASSERIE

Brasserie Flo Nice (▷ 66)
Brasserie La Rotonde (▷ 54)
La Canne à Sucre (▷ 54)
Le Caveau 30 (▷ 105)
Le Cenac (▷ 66)
La Ferme Saleya (▷ 39)
Les Jardins du Capitole (▷ 54)
Le Tire Bouchon (▷ 40)

## CAFÉS

Café des Musées (▷ 106)
Le Café de Paris (▷ 106)
Fenocchio (▷ 39)

## FINE DINING

Bar Boeuf et Co (▷ 106)
Bleu Citron (▷ 54)
Le Caprice (▷ 54)
Chantecler (▷ 54)
Château de la Chèvre d'Or (▷ 106)
La Colombe d'Or (▷ 106)
Don Camillo (▷ 39)
Le Festival (▷ 105)
Indyana (▷ 66)
Keisuke Matsushima (▷ 66)
Le Louis XV (▷ 106)
Luc Salsedo (▷ 68)
La Palme d'Or (▷ 105)
Restaurant Boccaccio (▷ 68)
Restaurant Stéphane Viano (▷ 68)
Le Saint Paul (▷ 106)
L'Univers de Christian Plumail (▷ 68)

## NICE/ITALIAN

La Baie d'Amalfi (▷ 66)
Restaurant du Gésu (▷ 40)

## NIÇOIS/PROVENÇAL

Les Agaves (▷ 105)
Chez Palmyre (▷ 39)
Chez René Socca (▷ 39)
Côté Jardin (▷ 105)
Les Épicuriens (▷ 66)
L'Estocaficada (▷ 39)
La Feniera (▷ 39)
Fleur de Sel (▷ 105)
Josy-Jo (▷ 105)
Lou Nissart (▷ 68)
La Merenda (▷ 40)
La Petite Biche (▷ 68)
La Petite Maison (▷ 40)

## SEAFOOD

Aphrodite (▷ 66)
Bacon (▷ 105)
Beau Rivage Plage (▷ 54)
Le Grand Café de Turin (▷ 40)
La Mère Germaine (▷ 106)

## SPANISH

Mireille (▷ 68)

## VEGETARIAN

La Zucca Magica (▷ 40)

## WINE BAR

La Part des Anges (▷ 68)

# If You Like...

However you'd like to spend your time in Nice, these top suggestions should help you tailor your ideal visit. Each sight or listing has a fuller write-up in Nice by Area.

## TASTY MEMORIES

**Box up some *navettes*** and flavoured biscuits from La Cure Gourmande (▷ 36).
**Taste some local olive oils** and choose the best for your kitchen at À l'Olivier (▷ 36).
**Buy a bottle of Nice's own Bellet wine** at Cave Caprioglio (▷ 36).

## ARTFUL SOUVENIRS

**Choose some Picasso-designed pottery** at the Galerie Madoura (▷ 102), in Vallauris.
**Buy some bubble glass** from the Verrerie de Biot (▷ 101), in Biot.

*Calisson sweets (top) or pottery from Vallauris (above) make good souvenirs*

## TRYING LOCAL FOOD

**Dine alfresco** with a plate of gnocchi at Restaurant du Gésu (▷ 40).
**Have a slice of *socca*** from Chez René Socca (▷ 39).
**Savour the *boeuf en daube*** at La Feniera (▷ 39).

## TOP TABLES

**Go for the Michelin stars** at Chantecler (▷ 54), Keisuke Matsushima (▷ 66), L'Univers de Christian Plumail (▷ 68) and Le Louis XV (▷ 106).
**Have a romantic meal** *à deux* on the terrace at Le Saint Paul (▷ 106).
**See and be seen** at super-chef Alain Ducasse's Bar Boeuf et Co (▷ 106), in Monaco.

*Traditional socca from Chez Thérésa (above right); there are plenty of options for fine dining in Nice and the surrounding area (right)*

*A night of jazz; the Aquarium in Monaco (below)*

## NIGHTLIFE

**Visit during the jazz festivals** in Nice or Antibes Juan-les-Pins (▷ 114, 96).
**Fire up the hot salsa** at La Bodeguita del Havana (▷ 65).
**Sip the cocktail of the month** at Hôtel Negresco's Relais bar (▷ 53).
**Roll the dice in style** at the Casino de Monte-Carlo (▷ 92).

## FAMILY FUN

**Enter a water world** at Monaco's Aquarium (▷ 91).
**Play a game of *osselets*** at the Musée Archéologique (▷ 77).
**Ride the carousel** in Jardin Albert I (▷ 62).
**Relax on a private beach** along the Promenade des Anglais (▷ 48–49).

## FREEBIES

**Municipal museums** are free on the first and third Sundays of each month.
**Take a free tour of the candy factory** at Confiserie Florian (▷ 36) and the perfumeries at Grasse (▷ 89).
**People-watch** in the parks and gardens of the Promenade du Paillon (▷ 62).
**Travel the Côte d'Azur by bus**—not quite free but a real bargain (▷ 118).

*The Fragonard perfume museum and factory in Grasse (above)*

*View of Nice from the Colline du Château (below)*

## BIRD'S-EYE VIEWS

**Survey Nice's red rooftops** from the viewpoints on the Colline du Château (▷ 25).
**Be dazzled** by the dramatic coastal views from Èze village (▷ 87).
**Enjoy the panoramic views** from the Grimaldi Castle tower at Haut-de-Cagnes (▷ 86).
**Climb the Saracen tower** at Cannes for stupendous views over the harbour (▷ 85).

ESSENTIAL NICE IF YOU LIKE...

## GREEN SPACES

**Stroll through** the tranquil monastery gardens in Cimiez (▷ 78).

**Enjoy the breezy air** and splendid views on top of the Colline du Château (▷ 25).

**Marvel at the strange succulents** and cacti in Monaco's Jardin Exotique (▷ 91).

**Dance to the musical fountains** of Villa Ephrussi's French gardens (▷ 93).

**Visit the lush gardens** of Menton (▷ 96).

*Fountains and flowers at the Villa Ephrussi (below)*

## UNFORGETTABLE WALKS

**Take in the atmosphere** on the Promenade des Anglais (▷ 48–49).

**Celebrity-spot** along La Croisette at Cannes (▷ 84).

**Circle St-Paul-de-Vence** along its medieval walls (▷ 98).

**Wander through the olive grove** at the Parc des Arènes (▷ 76–77) in Cimiez and into the monastery gardens at the northern end.

*Strolling along La Croisette, in Cannes (below)*

## ARTISTS OF THE RIVIERA

**Follow the Painters' Route** on the Côte d'Azur (▷ Tip, 82).

**Admire the ancient olive grove** at Renoir's house, at Cagnes-sur-Mer (▷ 86).

**Interpret Chagall's Biblical Message** at the Musée Marc Chagall (▷ 74–75).

**Visit the Musée Henri Matisse** (▷ 72–73) and his masterpiece, the Chapelle du Rosaire (▷ 99).

**See the whimsical Cocteau chapel** in Villefranche-sur-Mer (▷ 94) and his marriage salon in Menton (▷ 96).

MUSÉE MATISSE

*The Chapelle du Rosaire (above), at Vence, was decorated by Matisse, whose museum (left) is in Nice*

# Nice by Area

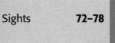

Nice's old town—Vieille Ville—is the heart and soul of the city. Restaurants and cafés spill out into lively squares, and the narrow streets are lined with shops and art galleries. Colline du Château, or Castle Hill, rises between the old town and the port.

**6**

**7**

**8**

**9**

Garibaldi

PLACE
GARIBALDI

BOULEVARD JEAN JAURÈS

Rue Neuve

Rue Saint-François

Rue Saint-Joseph

Rue Pairolière

Rue Saint-Augustin

RUE CATHERINE SÉGURANE

Montée

**Rue
Droite**

Chapelle de la
Sainte Croix

Cathédrale
Vieille Ville

Rue du Collet

Rue Sainte-Claire

Montée Menica Rondelly

Cimitière
Israëlite

**Palais Lascaris**

Place
Rossetti

Place
St-François

Rue de la Boucherie

Rue Centrale

Rue de la Loge

Rue Benoit Bunico

Rue Rossetti

Place du
Jésus

Rue Jésus

Église du Jésus

Rue du Château

Montée du Château

Allée des Justes

**Cathédrale
Sainte-Réparate**

Opéra
Vieille Ville

Palais
Rusca

**Palais de
Justice**

Rue de l'Abbaye

Rue de la Préfecture

Rue du Marché

Rue de la Place Vieille

**VIEILLE VILLE**

**Colline du
Château**

**Église Notre Dame
de l'Annonciation**

Hôtel de
Ville

Descente Crotti

Rue
Alexandre
Mari

Rue St-Gaëtan

Rue St-Joseph

Chapelle de la
Très-Sainte Trinité
et du St-Suaire

**Chapelle de la
Miséricorde**

Église St Dominique
et St François de Paule

Rue de l'Hôtel de Ville

Rue de l'Opéra

Rue Saint-François de Paule

**Cours
Saleya**

Rue de la
Barillerie

Cours Saleya

Cité du Parc

Cours Saleya

Cité du Parc

**Opéra
de Nice**

Rue
Milton
Robbins

**Galerie des
Ponchettes**

**Galerie
de la Marine**

**Tour
Bellanda**

Rue
Droubin

Rue Van Loo

Rue Bréa

Rue Sulzer

**PROMENADE DES ANGLAIS**

**QUAI DES ETATS-UNIS**

Rue des Ponchettes

Plage
Beau Rivage

Plage
de l'Opéra

Plage des
Ponchettes

Plage de
Castel

**QUAI RAUBA-CAPEU**

Monument
aux Morts

0        200 m
0        200 yds

**G**                    **H**

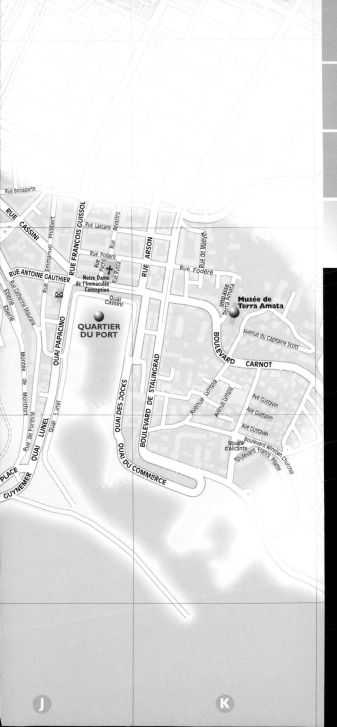

Rue Bonaparte

RUE CASSINI

RUE ANTOINE GAUTHIER

Eberlé

Eberlé

Rue Catherine Ségurane

Montée de Montfort

Rue de Foresta

Rue Emmanuel Philibert

RUE FRANÇOIS GUISSOL

Rue Lascaris

Rue Bavastro

Rue Fodéré

Rue Pacho

Rue Rusca

Notre Dame de l'Immaculée Conception

RUE ARSON

Rue de Maëvès

Rue Fodéré

Impasse Terra Amata

**Musée de Terra Amata**

Quai Cassini

Avenue du Capitaine Scott

**QUARTIER DU PORT**

QUAI PAPACINO

QUAI DES DOCKS

BOULEVARD DE STALINGRAD

BOULEVARD CARNOT

Avenue Urbino

Avenue Urbino

Ave Gustavin

Ave Gustavin

Ave Gustavin

Square d'Alicante

Boulevard Winston Churchill

Boulevard Franck Pilatte

Quai Lunel

QUAI LUNEL

QUAI DU COMMERCE

PLACE GUYNEMER

J

K

# Cathédrale Sainte-Réparate

*The eye-catching mosaic dome (left); inside, looking towards the altar (right)*

VIEILLE VILLE ★ TOP 25

## THE BASICS

- H7
- Place Rossetti
- 04 93 62 34 40
- Daily 8.30–noon, 2–6
- Cafés in place Rossetti
- All buses to Gare Routière
- Good
- Free

## HIGHLIGHTS

- Mosaic tiled dome
- Bell tower
- Marble high altar
- Marble choir stall balustrade
- St. Réparate's chapel
- Large organ
- Walnut panelling in the sacristy
- Baroque music concerts

**With its bell tower and tiled dome peeking out above the narrow streets, this monument to Nice's patron saint watches over one of the old town's liveliest squares and is an integral part of the life of the city.**

**Teenage martyr** The cathedral is dedicated to the city's patroness, St. Réparate, who was martyred for her faith in Palestine when she was just 15 years old. According to legend, after she was beheaded her body was carried away across the sea to Nice in a boat guarded by three angels. This is one explanation for how the Baie des Anges (Bay of Angels) got its name. St. Réparate's chapel is the first on the left as you enter the cathedral. Her story is depicted in a large painting between two marble pillars above the altar. Beneath it, a glass and gold reliquary supposedly contains one of the saint's bones.

**Main features** Built in the mid-17th century by Jean-André Guibera, a local architect, the cathedral is baroque in style. It is crowned by a striking mosaic dome of green and gold tiles. The slender bell tower soaring alongside dates from the 18th century. The ornate façade, with decorative capitals, niches, statuary and arcaded doorway, was added in 1825 and looks especially beautiful lit up at night. Inside, the spacious nave keeps the baroque decor of marble, stucco and gilt from becoming too excessive, while stained-glass windows high in the dome let in soft light. Concerts of baroque and classical music are sometimes held in this atmospheric setting.

*Steps leading up from the seafront (left); greenery around the waterfall (right)*

# Colline du Château

**Nice's first residents settled on this high green hill for security. Today people come to this sprawling park for its shady walks, breezy air and splendid views over the city, port and Baie des Anges.**

**Early foundations** Nice was founded on this site by the ancient Greeks, who established a trading post in the 4th century BC. They called it Nikaïa, which means 'victory'. The 90m (295ft) heights of the *colline* (hill) provided a natural lookout to watch for pirates and other invaders by land or sea. A medieval fortress—*le château*—withstood several sieges but was finally destroyed by Louis XIV's forces in the early 18th century. All that remains of it today are a few ruins along the fortification wall and the name, Castle Hill.

**On the heights** The Colline du Château is now a public park covering 19ha (47 acres). Also on the grounds are the ruins of an 11th- to 12th-century Romanesque church. Steep steps lead up from the old town or from the seafront along quai des États-Unis. Here you can also take the *ascenseur* (elevator) beside Tour Bellanda, which now houses a historical museum (▷ 34). At the top, meandering paths lead to spectacular viewpoints over the old town, port and coastline. On the port side, look for the pretty pebble mosaics along the path, or watch the pétanque players amid the crisp scent of mature pines. There's also children's playground, sports grounds, souvenir shops, cafés and even a waterfall leading back down towards Vieille Ville.

## THE BASICS

+ J7
- Between Vieille Ville and the Quartier du Port
- ☎ 04 93 85 62 33
- Apr, May, Sep daily 8–7; Jun–end Aug daily 8–8; Oct–end Mar daily 8–6
- Cafés, Brasserie La Table des Anges
- All buses to Gare Routière
- Good
- Free; *ascenseur* inexpensive
- *Ascenseur* operates Jun–end Aug daily 9–8; Apr, May, Sep daily 9–7; Oct–end Mar daily 10–6

## HIGHLIGHTS

- The views
- Tour Bellanda
- Cool breezes
- Shady strolls
- The waterfall

**VIEILLE VILLE**

**TOP 25**

# Cours Saleya

**Cours Saleya is much more than the site of Nice's famous flower market. It's where the locals come for a morning coffee in the sun, an ice cream or a summer evening stroll.**

**First promenade** Cours Saleya was Nice's first public promenade. Mulberry trees were planted here in 1668, and replaced by elms a century later. Today, lime trees grow between the market stalls, their blossoms giving off a sweet scent in the spring breeze. In 1861, the town's fruit and vegetable market moved here from place aux Herbes and place Rossetti. The flower market was established at this time.

**Along the Cours** From Tuesday to Saturday, the flower market runs through the middle of the l

*Market time in Cours Saleya: there's a flower market from Tuesday to Saturday, an antiques/flea market on Monday and a fruit and vegetable market at place Pierre*

wide esplanade. An antiques/flea market sets up here on Monday. Cafés and restaurants line either side of the market, providing good vantage points for people-watching. You can walk right through the heart of the market, admiring the beautiful displays—and the low prices. Carnations are the speciality of the region. At place Pierre Gauthier, flowers give way to a sumptuous fruit and vegetable market piled high with local produce, including herbs, olives and home-made cheeses and honey.

**The sights** If they're open, stop in to see the lovely baroque Chapelle de la Miséricorde (▷ 33) and the Chapelle du St-Suaire (▷ 31). The striking yellow building at the Cours' eastern end is where Matisse set up his studio when he first came to Nice.

## THE BASICS

➕ H7
✉ Cours Saleya
🕐 Flower market Tue–Sat 7–4; produce market Tue–Sun 7–1; antiques market Mon 7.30–6
🍴 Cafés and restaurants
🚌 All buses to Gare Routière
♿ Good
🖐 Free

VIEILLE VILLE

★

TOP 25

# Palais Lascaris

*Flemish tapestries and an ornately frescoed ceiling (left); detail of a fresco (right)*

## THE BASICS

✚ H7
✉ 15 rue Droite
☎ 04 93 62 72 40
🕐 Wed–Mon 10–6
🚌 All buses to Gare Routière
♿ None
🎫 Free

## HIGHLIGHTS

● 18th-century pharmacy
● Musical instrument collection
● Tapestries in the Grand Salon (second floor)
● *Venus and Adonis* ceiling fresco (second floor)
● Lavish bedchamber decor

**Visit this splendid baroque mansion for a rare glimpse of upper-class life in the Vieille Ville in the 17th and 18th centuries. Highlights include a period pharmacy and fashionable musical instruments such as the *viole d'amour*.**

**Hidden grandeur** It's easy to walk right past the unassuming façade of Palais Lascaris, its grey stone exterior hemmed in between the shops of rue Droite. But step inside and a monumental marble staircase leads from the ornate inner court-yard, with its vaulted, frescoed ceiling, to four floors of baroque splendour. Built in 1648, the Genoese-style palace was home to the Lascaris-Vintimiglia family. In a side room off the entrance hall, an apothecary's shop dating from 1738 has been installed.

**Ancient music** In 2009 Palais Lascaris will become the city's music museum. Based on the collection of Antoine Gautier, an amateur musician born in Nice in 1825, it will contain some 382 instruments from Europe, Africa, China and Japan. It represents the second-biggest collection of ancient instruments in France. Many instruments are already displayed on the first floor, including a pianoforte, mandolin and *viole d'amour*, a stringed instrument fashionable in the 18th century. It was said at the time that of all the instruments, the *viole d'amour* approached most closely the sound of the human voice. The second floor is filled with beautiful tapestries, baroque furniture, statues, lavish plasterwork and ceiling frescoes.

*Boats moored at the port (left); honouring the victims of World War I (right)*

**The old port of Nice is a picturesque sight. On its eastern side, the tall Italian façades painted in bright shades of red, pink and yellow make a wonderful backdrop for the luxurious yachts that fill the marina.**

**Plenty to see** The port culminates in the rectangular Bassin Lympia east of the Vieille Ville. In the Vigier Gardens, on the port's eastern flank, the Canary Island date palm was first acclimatised in 1864. It is now common all along the Riviera. On the west side, the Colline du Château (▷ 25) rises above busy quai Lunel, lined with restaurants and shops, including the delectable Confiserie Florian (▷ 36), which produces crystallized fruits and flower petals. A huge memorial at the base of the hill, the Monument aux Morts, honours the 4,000 Niçois who died in World War I. Keeping watch at the head of the harbour is the Church of Immaculate Conception, also called Our Lady of the Port, where sailors came for blessings before dangerous journeys.

**Dredging deep** Nice had no port in medieval times; ships simply dropped anchor on the other side of the Colline du Château, around the windy headland known locally as Rauba Capeu (Stolen Cap). In 1750 the Duke of Savoy decided to excavate a deep-water port to increase trade. But despite decades of work, it never really took off. Today the port is used mainly for fishing and pleasure craft, and by ferries sailing to Corsica. Big cruise ships use the deeper port at Villefranche (▷ 94).

**THE BASICS**

➕ J7
🍴 A choice of cafés and restaurants
🚌 9, 10, 20

**HIGHLIGHTS**

● Bright façades
● Vigier Gardens
● Antiques shopping in Village Ségurane (▷ 37)
● Confiserie Florian (▷ 36)

**VIEILLE VILLE**

★

**TOP 25**

# Vieille Ville

## HIGHLIGHTS

- Chapelle de la Miséricorde
- Rue Droite
- An ice cream in place Rossetti
- Browsing in the shops and galleries
- Dining outdoors

### TIP

- There are many ice-cream vendors in the Vieille Ville, but none can surpass Fenocchio (▷ 39), in place Rossetti. Its 96 flavours range from old favourites like mint chocolate to lavender and flower-scented *parfums* and such unusual tastes as beer, tomato and chilli pepper.

**In Nice's old town you can window shop along narrow streets, explore baroque churches, or relax at an outdoor table with a drink or an alfresco meal.**

**Medieval streets** The atmospheric streets of the Vieille Ville wind between the curving triangle bounded by place Garibaldi at the tip, boulevard Jean Jaurès on the west and the Colline du Château on the east. On the southern side, the quai des États-Unis runs alongside the sea and Les Ponchettes beach. Some buildings date back to the 14th century. The bright façades reflect the architectural styles and colours that flourished in old Nice under the Counts of Savoy, especially the deep ochre hue known as *rouge sarde* (Sardinian red). Street signs in Vieille Ville are in two languages: French on top and *Nissart* below.

*Clockwise from left: shops in rue de la Préfecture; the clock tower in place du Palais; an outdoor café in place Rossetti; ornate street lamps and shuttered windows typical of the Vieille Ville*

**Baroque brilliance** The Vieille Ville's two main thoroughfares are rue Droite (▷ 34) and Cours Saleya (▷ 26–27). From the latter, walk through the arcades to the Galerie des Ponchettes (▷ 33) and the Galerie de la Marine (▷ 33). The beautiful baroque churches are a highlight of the old town. The Cathédrale Sainte-Réparate (▷ 24) towers over place Rossetti, the lively main square. But it's worth seeking out the smaller baroque gems, when they're open. These include the Chapelle de la Miséricorde (▷ 33), Église Notre Dame de l'Annonciation (▷ 33) and Église St-Jacques (▷ rue Droite, 34). Many chapels, such as the Chapelle de la Très-Sainte Trinité and the adjoining Chapelle du St-Suaire (Holy Shroud), on rue Jules Gilly, are attached to the medieval penitents, or brotherhoods, who once held important responsibilities in the city.

**THE BASICS**

✚ H7
🍴 Many cafes and restaurants
🚌 All buses to Gare Routière

31

## More to See

### CHAPELLE DE LA MISÉRICORDE

Dating from 1740 and belonging to the Brotherhood of Black Penitents, this beautiful baroque chapel is resplendent with coloured marble pillars, gold capitals and crystal chandeliers. Murals of saints and angels cover every surface, with notable works by Louis Bréa.

➕ H7 ✉ Cours Saleya ⏱ Tue 2.30–5pm
🚌 All buses to Gare Routière ⚿ Few
👆 Free

### ÉGLISE NOTRE DAME DE L'ANNONCIATION

Another baroque gem, with lovely skylit murals and rose marble pillars, this church is dedicated to St. Rita, the patron of hopeless causes, whose chapel is on the left as you enter.

➕ H7 ✉ Rue de la Poissonnerie
⏱ Mon–Sat 7–noon, 2.30–6, Sun 8–noon, 3–6.30 🚌 All buses to Gare Routière
⚿ Few 👆 Free

### GALERIE DE LA MARINE

The Galerie de la Marine is one of two galleries in the old fishmarket along the seafront and it specializes in modern art exhibitions by local artists.

➕ H7 ✉ 59 quai des États-Unis
☎ 04 93 62 37 11 ⏱ Tue–Sun 10–6; closed 1 Jan, Easter Sunday, 1 May, Christmas
🚌 All buses to Gare Routière ⚿ Few
👆 Free

### GALERIE DES PONCHETTES

Henri Matisse persuaded the city to turn the old fishmarket into gallery space for changing art exhibitions. The arched spaces along the walls are a perfect backdrop for large works of art. Several exhibitions are held here each year, usually of contemporary art.

➕ G7 ✉ 77 quai des États-Unis ☎ 04 93 62 31 24 ⏱ Tue–Sun 10–6; closed 1 Jan, Easter Sunday, 1 May, Christmas 🚌 All buses to Gare Routière ⚿ Few 👆 Free

### MUSÉE DE TERRA AMATA

www.musee-terra-amata.org

To the east of the port, this paleontology museum was built on a site occupied by prehistoric hunters 400,000 years ago. Exhibits include a footprint, tools, fire remains and

*Viewing the exhibits in the Galerie des Ponchettes (above); La Barque Bleue restaurant, in the Quartier du Port (left)*

*The baroque façade of the Chapelle de la Miséricorde*

exhibits on life in these ancient times.
➕ K7 ✉ 25 boulevard Carnot
☎ 04 93 55 59 93 🕐 Tue–Sun 10–6;
closed 1 Jan, Easter Sunday, 1 May, Christmas
🚌 30, 32A ♿ Good 💷 Moderate

## OPÉRA DE NICE

www.opera-nice.org
Rebuilt in 1885 after a disastrous fire,
the Opéra was styled after Paris'
Opéra Palais Garnier and is a grand
example of Nice's belle-époque architecture. This landmark has entertained
royalty, from Napoleon III to Tsar
Alexander II and Ludwig II of Bavaria.
➕ G7 ✉ 4–6 rue St-François-de-Paule
☎ 04 92 17 40 00 🕐 Open only for
performances 🚌 All buses to Gare Routière
♿ None

## PALAIS DE JUSTICE

Dominating the wide, pedestrian place
du Palais, these neoclassical law
courts were built in the late 19th
century. In the evening, their broad
steps are a meeting place for young
people before a night out in the old
town. Across the square is the pink

clock tower of Palais Rusca, a former
barracks turned courthouse annex.
➕ H7 ✉ Place du Palais 🚌 All buses to
Gare Routière

## RUE DROITE

Many French medieval cities had a 'rue
Droite'—literally the direct route
through town from gate to gate. This
one is lined with galleries and boutiques. Pop in to Église St-Jacques,
known as Le Gesu, to see its trompe-
l'oeil ceiling and profusion of angel
statuary. At No. 28 is Chez Thérésa,
where you can watch traditional *socca*
being made through the open window.
➕ H7 🚌 All buses to Gare Routière

## TOUR BELLANDA

Tour Bellanda, the 19th-century tower
on the Colline du Château (▷ 25), is
a delightful setting for the changing art
and history exhibitions of the Castle
Hill Historical Museum.
➕ H8 ✉ Colline du Château ☎ 04 93 85
62 33 🕐 Tue–Sun 10–6; closed 1 Jan, Easter
Sunday, 1 May, Christmas 🚌 All buses to
Gare Routière ♿ Few 💷 Free

*The belle-époque Opéra de Nice*

*An art gallery on the rue Droite*

# A Medieval Meander

Wander through the old town's medieval streets, soaking up the atmosphere of its busy squares, baroque churches and art galleries.

**DISTANCE:** 2km (1.25 miles) **ALLOW:** 2 hours

**START**

**COURS SALEYA** (▷ 26–27)
✚ H7 🚌 All buses to Gare Routière

**1** Starting at the western end of Cours Saleya, walk through the flower market. You will pass the Chapelle de la Miséricorde (▷ 33), on your left. Stop in if it's open.

**2** Continue to the place Charles Félix and admire the tall yellow building where Henri Matisse had his studio.

**3** Turn left on rue Jules Gilly, with the Chapelle de la Très-Sainte Trinité and Chapelle du St-Suaire on your right. Cross the tiny place de l'Ancien Senat and rue Préfecture, and carry straight ahead into rue Droite (▷ 34).

**4** Take your time along rue Droite, browsing in the many shops and art galleries. Visit the lovely baroque church of Le Gesu. At No. 28, on the corner with rue Rossetti, watch them making *socca* through the open window at Chez Thérésa.

**END**

**COURS SALEYA**
✚ H7 🚌 All buses to Gare Routière

**8** Retrace your steps to the junction and bear left down rue Droite, where you can visit more galleries and the Palais Lascaris (▷ 28). At rue Rossetti, turn left for the steps up to the Colline du Château (▷ 25), or continue straight on to Cours Saleya.

**7** Rue de Collet soon ends at a small triangular junction. Bear left up rue St-François to place St-François, where a fountain with four dolphins is surrounded by a boisterous morning fish market.

**6** From the adjoining place Halle aux Herbes, turn right up rue Mascoinat into the narrow maze of streets. Take the right-hand fork past Maison de la Pizza. When rue Mascoinat joins rue Central at a wide junction, bear right up rue de Collet.

**5** Turn left and walk down to place Rossetti. After visiting the cathedral, linger in the square over a drink or an ice cream from Fenocchio (▷ 39).

# Shopping

## À L'OLIVIER

This family-run shop has been in business since 1922 and sells a tempting array of olive oils, including oils flavoured with truffle, ginger, lemon or chestnut. It also sells vinegars, jams, spices and other items.

🔲 G7 ✉ 7 rue St-François-de-Paule ☎ 04 93 13 44 97 🚌 All buses to Gare Routière

## ART-DAC

www.art-dac.com
English artist Dean A. Clark produces attractive, sometimes dreamy, landscapes, and almost-abstract portraits and nudes.

🔲 H7 ✉ 10 rue Droite ☎ 04 93 53 91 10 🚌 All buses to Gare Routière

## AU TOMBEAU DE LA VAISSELLE

All kinds of items for wining and dining—from cooking gadgets to corkscrews and bar accessories.

🔲 H7 ✉ 3 place St-François ☎ 04 93 85 84 10 🚌 All buses to Gare Routière

## BALADE EN PROVENCE

The bright yellows, blues and greens of Provence leap out from this shop, which sells olive oils, jams, mustards, liqueurs and many other regional food and craft items. They make good souvenirs too.

🔲 H7 ✉ Rue du Collet ☎ 04 93 62 44 37 🚌 All buses to Gare Routière

## CAVE CAPRIOGLIO

This wonderful old wine shop was founded in 1910, and stocks everything from rare bottles to wine by the litre.

🔲 H7 ✉ 16 rue de la Préfecture ☎ 04 93 85 66 57 🚌 All buses to Gare Routière

## CENTRE D'ART HAITIEN

Unusual metal sculptures, paintings, mirrors, wall hangings and carvings can be found in this gallery of Haitian art.

🔲 H7 ✉ 35 rue Droite ☎ 06 09 52 89 06 🚌 All buses to Gare Routière

## LE CHANDELIER

This shop specializes in candles. Large, small, decorative, plain—there's sure to be something that catches your eye.

🔲 H7 ✉ 7 rue de la Boucherie ☎ 04 93 85 85 19 🚌 All buses to Gare Routière

### OLD TOWN MARKETS

There are various Saturday markets held in the place du Palais de Justice, on the southern edge of the old town, usually from 7am–7pm (5pm in winter). On the first and fourth Saturdays of the month is an antique book market, on the first, third and fourth Saturdays an artists' market, and on the first, second and third Saturdays a market for stamps, coins, picture postcards and various other collectables.

## CLAIR OBSCUR

www.pierres-bijoux.com
Jewellery and stones from Madagascar are the focus of this shop.

🔲 H7 ✉ 9 rue Droite ☎ 04 93 80 44 27 🚌 All buses to Gare Routière

## CONFISERIE FLORIAN

www.confiserieflorian.com
The old Nice candy factory beside the port is now home to Confiserie Florian, which specializes in crystallized fruits and flower petals. You can see the items being made and then choose from the extensive range of products in the upstairs gift shop.

🔲 J7 ✉ 14 quai Papacino ☎ 04 93 55 43 50 🚌 9, 10, 20

## LA CURE GOURMANDE

www.la-cure-gourmande.com
Anyone with a sweet tooth should love this shop, with its delicious biscuits and sweets from the region. You buy a decorative box and then fill it up with your biscuits of choice.

🔲 H7 ✉ 2 rue Sainte Réparate ☎ 04 93 62 41 78 🚌 All buses to Gare Routière

## DIAGRAM

Objects old and new, including jewellery and glassware, from China, Japan, Korea and other parts of the Far East.

🔲 H7 ✉ 11 Cours Saleya ☎ 04 93 80 33 71 🚌 All buses to Gare Routière

### THE EARTH COLLECTION

The lovely clothing range sold here is made from natural fibres, such as silk and cotton, in white, beige or pastel tones of pink and blue. There are branches in other Riviera towns, too.

🔁 H7 ✉ 10 rue Centrale ☎ 04 93 85 70 02 🚌 All buses to Gare Routière

### ETNOSUD

This shop specializes in items from Indonesia and Thailand—everything from furniture to smaller decorative objects.

🔁 J7 ✉ 15 rue François Guissol ☎ 04 93 56 08 36 🚌 30

### LOU CANICE

The shop window displays the traditional Provençal biscuits, *navettes*, in a wide variety of flavours, which make a good gift if you can resist temptation long enough to get them home.

🔁 H7 ✉ 7 rue Mascoïnat ☎ 04 93 85 41 62 🚌 All buses to Gare Routière

### MARCHÉ AUX FLEURS

One of Nice's unmissable attractions is its flower market, when Cours Saleya fills with stalls packed with the colours and scents of Provence, including, in season, spectacular sunflowers.

🔁 H7 ✉ Cours Saleya 🕐 Tue–Sat 7–4 🚌 All buses to Gare Routière

### MOLINARD

www.molinard.com

This delightful Nice branch of the Molinard perfume factory not only has the usual fine range of perfumes for women, but there are also scents for men and for children, as well as a small perfume museum at the back of the shop.

🔁 G7 ✉ 20 rue St-François-de-Paule ☎ 04 93 62 90 50 🚌 All buses to Gare Routière

### MOULIN À HUILE ALZIARI

A Nice institution, this shop has been owned by the same family for years. It sells top-quality olive oils and related products, as well, of course, as olives, from the family farms.

🔁 G7 ✉ 14 rue St-François-de-Paule ☎ 04 93 85 76 92 🚌 All buses to Gare Routière

### MICHEL JARRY GALLERY

If you visit only one shop in the winding streets of the old town, make it this one, at 12 rue de la Loge. It features the remarkable work of sculptor Michel Jarry, who creates magic out of metal, including wonderfully detailed little peacocks complete with tail feathers made out of spoons and the handles of old scissors. Jarry has his workshop next door, and you can watch him create his fascinating and truly original works of art.

### OLIVIERA

www.oliviera.com

The friendly owner here loves his olive oil and wines, and will provide you with free tastings of oils from all around the Mediterranean. The shop also has a lovely little eating area where you can enjoy a simple menu that makes the most of the oils.

🔁 H7 ✉ 8 bis rue du Collet ☎ 04 93 13 06 45 🚌 All buses to Gare Routière

### TERRE DES TRUFFES

This is the shop for truffle hounds, selling not only the truffles themselves but also products such as truffle cream, truffle oil and truffle paste—not cheap, but hard to resist.

🔁 G7 ✉ 11 rue St-François-de-Paule ☎ 04 93 62 07 68 🚌 All buses to Gare Routière

### TRANSPARENCE

This little gift shop sells attractive jewellery, as well as ships and other items embedded in glass cubes—they may sound odd but they are unusual and attractive.

🔁 H7 ✉ 2 rue Gilly ☎ 06 21 54 64 83 🚌 All buses to Gare Routière

### VILLAGE SÉGURANE

There are 40 antique shops and galleries in this antiques 'village' by the port, selling clocks, rustic French furniture and other collectable items.

🔁 J7 ✉ Rue Catherine Ségurane 🚌 1, 2 and others

# Entertainment and Nightlife

## BAR DES OISEAUX

www.bardesoiseaux.com
Founded by Nice actress and comedienne Noëlle Perna, who performs in the 50-seat theatre here when her schedule allows, Bar des Oiseaux is also a bar-cum-restaurant, where there are jazz performances and a gathering of Niçois intellectuals.
✚ H7 ✉ 5 rue St-Vincent
☎ 04 93 80 27 33
🕐 Daily lunch, dinner 🚌 All buses to Gare Routière

## CASA DEL SOL

Wrought iron, red and ochre decor, soft lights and big comfortable armchairs set the scene at this restaurant and lounge bar. There's trendy music, DJs and dancing from 11pm.
✚ H8 ✉ 69 quai des Etats-Unis ☎ 04 93 62 87 28
🕐 Until 2.30am 🚌 All buses to Gare Routière

## DIZZY CLUB

Down at the port, below the Colline du Château, this club has a dance floor and live music, which ranges from jazz to rock or soul. It's always packed here, thanks partly to its reasonable drink prices.
✚ J8 ✉ 26 quai Lunel
☎ 04 93 26 54 79 🕐 Daily 8pm–2.30am 🚌 All buses to Gare Routière

## JOHNNY'S WINE BAR

Johnny is the host and occasional musician at this tiny but usually packed Canadian wine bar just up from place Rossetti and Fenocchio's (▷ 39). There are no spirits, just wine and beer and some of the cheapest prices in Nice—'Happy prices all the time' is their claim.
✚ H7 ✉ 1 rue Rossetti
☎ 04 93 80 65 97
🕐 Tue–Sun 4pm–12.30am
🚌 All buses to Gare Routière

## O'HARA'S TAVERN

With a wide range of British, Irish and other European beers, as well as English-language newspapers, O'Hara's is a popular hang-out early evening, then really gets going with live music sessions at night. Celtic cuisine is served, too.
✚ H7 ✉ 22 rue Droite
☎ 04 93 80 43 22 🕐 Daily 4pm–2.30am 🚌 All buses to Gare Routière

### MUSIC TO YOUR EARS

If you want to enjoy a drink while listening to music, there are several bars along the rue de la Préfecture that are busy every night. Most offer live music, but before sitting down, check what's on offer that night. Some nights it could just be a guitarist providing background music, and not always very well, while other nights it could be a great jazz group or an ear-splitting young rock band.

## OPÉRA DE NICE

www.opera-nice.org
If you think Nice's 19th-century opera house looks good from the outside, step inside to see the sumptuous interior, with chandeliers, sweeping stairs and general plushness. It hosts classical music concerts and dance performances.
✚ G7 ✉ 4 rue St-François-de-Paule ☎ 04 92 17 40 40
🕐 Box office Mon–Sat 9–6
🚌 All buses to Gare Routière

## PADDY'S PUB

www.paddyspub.fr
Paddy's is a very lively and popular Irish bar in the heart of the old town, where the low ceilings add to the noise level, as do the sports screens and the live music sessions held on several nights of the week. The place is packed on Celtic music evenings.
✚ H7 ✉ 40 rue Droite
☎ 04 93 80 06 75 🕐 Daily 4pm–2.30am 🚌 All buses to Gare Routière

## WAYNE'S

www.waynes.fr
If you want a wild time go to Wayne's, which attracts the good-time party crowd for live music nights with young bands, karaoke nights and party theme nights. Be prepared for anything outrageous.
✚ H7 ✉ 15 rue de la Préfecture ☎ 04 93 13 46 99
🕐 Daily noon–1am 🚌 All buses to Gare Routière

# Restaurants

VIEILLE VILLE

RESTAURANTS

## PRICES

Prices are approximate, based on a three-course meal for one person.

| | |
|---|---|
| €€€ | over €50 |
| €€ | €20–€50 |
| € | under €20 |

## CHEZ PALMYRE (€–€€)

This simple place has always been busy, but a rave review in the *New York Times* has now made reservations essential. It's unpretentious, and for the French it must be like walking into grandmother's kitchen. The menu changes daily depending on what's in the market. Whatever the daily specials, they'll be authentic Niçois dishes.

➕ H7 ✉ 5 rue Droite
☎ 04 93 92 05 73
🕐 Mon–Sat lunch, dinner
🚌 All buses to Gare Routière

## CHEZ RENÉ SOCCA (€)

Every visitor to Nice should dine here at least once to taste some of the best *socca* (▷ panel) in the city. Queue up to get your slice of freshly made *socca* (though there are lots of other dishes at another window) and take it to a table, then wash it down with a glass of local rosé wine.

➕ H7 ✉ 2 rue Miralheti
☎ 04 93 92 05 73
🕐 Tue–Sun 9am–10pm; closed Jan 🚌 All buses to Gare Routière

## DON CAMILLO (€€€)

Chef and former owner Stéphane Viano made this restaurant one of the essential dining experiences in Nice. Can his young replacement Laville Marc maintain the standards? Signs are that he can, with dishes such as langoustine sushi and a wonderful banana risotto dessert.

➕ H7 ✉ 5 rue des Ponchettes ☎ 04 93 85 67 95 🕐 Mon–Fri lunch, dinner, Sat dinner 🚌 All buses to Gare Routière

## L'ESTOCAFICADA (€€)

Several generations have cooked here, handing down family recipes including the one for the stockfish that gives the place its Provençal name.

➕ G7 ✉ 2 rue de l'Hôtel-de-Ville ☎ 04 93 80 21 64
🕐 Tue–Sat lunch, dinner
🚌 1, 2, 5

### FINGER FOOD

'Outdoors we eat with our fingers,' says a sign outside Chez René Socca, one of the most popular places in Nice for sampling the city's specialty: *socca*. *Socca* is chickpea flour mixed with olive oil and water. The pancake-like batter is then spread very thinly on a large copper pan, and baked in a wood-fired oven. *Socca* is inexpensive and can be eaten for breakfast, lunch, supper or as a snack.

## LA FENIERA (€€)

La Feniera has rustic Provençal decor, occasional music evenings and one of the best *boeuf en daube à la Niçoise* you're ever likely to taste.

➕ H7 ✉ 5 rue Mascoïnat
☎ 04 93 80 26 80
🕐 Wed–Sun lunch and dinner
🚌 All buses to Gare Routière

## FENOCCHIO (€)

By far the busiest eating place in town is Fenocchio, Nice's best ice-cream shop. Choose from 96 flavours (at the last count), including oddities like beer and chilli pepper, but also mouth-watering ones such as lavender and orange flower. It also serves crêpes, and there's a large outdoor seating area if you want to linger.

➕ H7 ✉ Place Rossetti
☎ 04 93 80 72 52 🕐 Daily 9am–midnight 🚌 All buses to Gare Routière

## LA FERME SALEYA (€€)

The whimsical farmyard decor gives this newish place a very friendly feel, and the food is superb. It ranges from *moules* and salads to mains like trout in almonds or fillet of beef cooked in roquefort, and the chef claims his tiramisu is the best in Nice!

➕ H7 ✉ 8 rue Jules Gilly
☎ 04 93 55 84 32
🕐 Mon–Sat lunch, dinner
🚌 All buses to Gare Routière

## LE GRAND CAFÉ DE TURIN (€€)

This popular brasserie is renowned for its seafood. Service can be a little chaotic, but customers are happy as long as they get their sea urchins, sea snails or oysters.

➕ J6 ✉ 5 place Garibaldi ☎ 04 93 62 29 52 🕐 Thu–Tue 8am–10pm; closed Wed 🚌 All buses to Gare Routière

## LA MERENDA (€€)

The Merenda is a Nice institution. It's small and has no phone, so you have to book in person. You also have to pay in cash, but the place is full every night with people enjoying the excellent local cuisine, like beef daube. Note there are only two sittings nightly, so be prompt.

➕ G7 ✉ 4 rue Raoul Bosio ☎ No phone 🕐 Mon–Fri, seatings at 7.15pm and 9.15pm 🚌 All buses to Gare Routière

## LA PETITE MAISON (€€)

This is where Nice high society comes for hearty and wonderful cooking. From politicians to musicians, everyone enjoys some of the best Niçois dishes in town. Start with the special plate of Niçois starters like *pissaladière* and take it from there—if you can get a table.

➕ G7 ✉ 11 rue St-François-de-Paule ☎ 04 93 85 71 53 🕐 Mon–Sat lunch, dinner 🚌 All buses to Gare Routière

## RESTAURANT DU GÉSU (€–€€)

One of the best old town dining experiences is in the large courtyard occupied by the Gésu. Waiters run frantically around, while people willingly wait half an hour for a table. The home-made gnocchi is one specialty, and the pizzas are popular too, but you can't really go wrong here.

➕ H7 ✉ 1 place du Jésus ☎ 04 93 62 26 46 🕐 Mon–Sat lunch, dinner 🚌 All buses to Gare Routière

## RESTAURANT PAMIR (€–€€)

www.restaurant-pamir.com Afghan cuisine in Nice? Why not when it's as good as the Pamir? There are a few tables on the balcony but much more space inside. It's a good menu for vegetarians, and one of the best

### NICE PIZZA

You will see *pissaladière* on many menus, usually as a starter. It is a kind of small, Provençal pizza with a thick doughy base. Unlike pizza, the *pissaladière* doesn't present you with a hundred different options, although versions of it do vary. The topping is made up of anchovies, olives and onions, which are fried until they are soft and melt in your mouth. Try it at least once, though once is seldom enough!

options for meat-eaters is the Afghan national dish, *Narenj Palao*—marinated veal and rice perfumed with orange zests, raisins, almonds and pistachio.

➕ H7 ✉ 3 rue Ste-Claire ☎ 04 93 80 83 49 🕐 Daily lunch, dinner 🚌 All buses to Gare Routière

## LE TIRE BOUCHON (€€)

Long-established place that ignores fashion and serves traditional dishes in a red-and-black velvet dining room. Dishes like lamb in garlic are simple but superb, and there's the relaxed atmosphere of a place that knows what it's doing.

➕ H7 ✉ 19 rue de la Préfecture ☎ 04 93 92 63 64 🕐 Daily dinner only 🚌 All buses to Gare Routière

## LA ZUCCA MAGICA (€€)

Down by the port, this vegetarian restaurant is a wonderfully friendly place, and you don't need to order as there's a set menu chosen by the chef each day. It's the kind of refreshing and inventive cooking that shows just how tasty vegetarian cuisine can be. The courses keep on coming, until you're ready to burst. Book ahead, go hungry and enjoy a meal to remember.

➕ J7 ✉ 4 bis quai Papacino ☎ 04 93 56 25 27 🕐 Tue–Sat lunch, dinner 🚌 1, 2, 9, 10

This breezy promenade, lined with palms and beautiful belle-époque hotels, is Nice's star attraction. It's a place to stroll, skate, sunbathe or enjoy an alfresco meal beside the beach. It runs the length of the water-front all the way to the airport.

**4**

**5**

**6**

**7**

Chemin des Collinettes

Avenue Robert Schum

Maeterlinck

Avenue Schuman

Boulevard de la Madeleine

Route de Bellet

Avenue Alexandre Ansaldi

Avenue Vaillant

Voie Pierre Mathis

Avenue

**Musée des Beaux-Arts**

**PIERRE MATHIS**

Musée Chéret

**VOIE**

Avenue Etienne

Rue Henri C

Avenue Rosa Bonneur

Boulevard Carlone

Rue Saint-Honoré

Résidence Universitaire Baie des Anges

Boulevard Edouard Herriot

Boulevard de Magnan

Rue Ernest Honoré

Rue Louis de Coppet

Avenue de Bellet

**8**

Boulevard Edouard Herriot

Avenue Aimé Martin

Boulevard Mont Rabeau

Avenue Aimé Martin

Avenue de Magnan

Tunnel de Magnan

**PROMENAD**

Chemin de Cimbra

Avenue du Mont

Avenue Piaget

Voie Pierre Mathis

Voie de la Californie

**TUNNEL DE MAGNAN**

Rue

Chemin des Crotes

Avenue du Mesnil

Avenue universitaire

Avenue Aimé Martin

Avenue de Fabron

**VOIE**

Avenue de la Californie

**Polyclinique Santa-Maria**

Bambou Plage

Chemin de l'Archet

Parc de Fabron

Avenue de Fabron

Indochine de

**PIERRE MATHIS**

Avenue de la Californie

**Hôpital Lenval**

**PROMENADE DES ANGLAIS**

**9**

**Musée International d'Art Naïf Anatoly Jakovsky**

**VOIE**

Miami Plage

**Musée des Arts Asiatiques, Parc Phoenix**

**A**     **B**     **C**

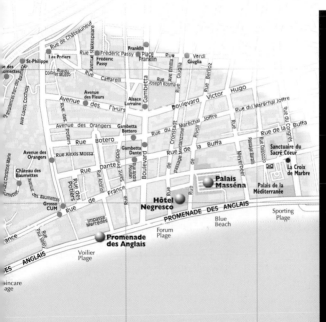

Rue de Chateauneuf

St-Philippe

Rue des
aumettes

Les Potiers

Rue du
Colbob Musso

Franklin

Frédéric Passy

Frédéric
Passy

Place
Franklin

Rue

Verdi
Giuglia

Rue des Potiers

Résidence Parc de Baumettes

Ave Louis Cochois

Avenue
des Fleurs

Caffarelli

Alsace
Lorraine

Avenue

des

Fleurs

Rue des Potiers

Rue Emilia

Rue
Joseph Kosma

Rue Giuglia

Gambetta

Rue Berlioz

Avenue Shakespeare

Boulevard

Victor

Hugo

Rue du Maréchal Joffre

Rue du Congrès

Avenue des Orangers

Gambetta
Bottero

Rue

Botero

Rue du

Maréchal Joffre

Rivoli

Rue

Rue de la Buffa

Buffa

Avenue des
Orangers

Rue Alexis Mossa

Gambetta
Dante

Rue de la Buffa

Passage Barla

Passage Dalpozzo

Rue Dalpozzo

Sanctuaire du
Sacré Coeur

av de Cristina Marie

Château des
Baumettes

Rue André Poulain

Cronstadt

Passage Raynaud

Meyerber

La Croix
de Marbre

Rue Dante

Boulevard

Rue de

Rue de

aumettes

Grosso
CUM

Rue Michiel

Rue

des

Potiers

Rue

de

France

Palais
Masséna

Palais de la
Méditerranée

France

Impasse
Mercèdes

Hôtel
Negresco

PROMENADE DES ANGLAIS

Sporting
Plage

ES

ANGLAIS

Rue
Paul Déroulède

Promenade
des Anglais

Forum
Plage

Blue
Beach

ance

Voilier
Plage

incare
age

0        250 m

0        250 yds

D        E        F

# Hôtel Negresco

## HIGHLIGHTS

- The domed façade
- Salon Royal
- Salon Versailles
- The walnut-panelled bar
- The lavish toilets
- The moving carousel horses in La Rotonde

**This landmark hotel symbolizes all the luxury and stylishness of the belle époque. Inside, its exquisite art and decoration were chosen by the owner to reveal the rich detail of different eras in French history.**

## TIP

- Hôtel Negresco isn't generally open to non-guests, but ask at reception and they may let you have a peek at the Salon Royal and other ground-floor rooms (dress appropriately). Or come for a meal (▷ 54).

**Riviera palace** Henri Negresco was born of humble origins in Bucharest and became a famous *maître d'hôtel*. He dreamed of building a palace on the Promenade des Anglais that would provide every luxury for rich and royal guests, and chose Edouard Niermans, one of the leading architects of the belle époque, to design it. Hôtel Negresco opened to great acclaim in 1913, but a year later World War I broke out and it was turned into a hospital. With his wealthy clientele decimated by the war, Negresco was ruined. He died in

*The belle-époque Hôtel Negresco is one of Nice's most famous buildings*

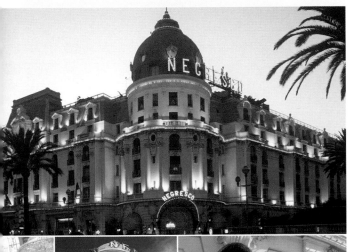

1920, aged 52. The hotel fell into decline until 1957, when the Augier family bought it and re-established its legendary splendour. Its famous guests range from rock stars to royalty.

**Private museum** Staying at the Negresco is a little like living in a sumptuous private museum. Madame Jeanne Augier has collected an impressive range of traditional and contemporary art. Each of the five floors has a specific decoration. All the rooms are different, most furnished with valuable antiques. The highlight, on the ground floor, is the sweeping Salon Royal, with its glass dome by Gustave Eiffel, Baccarat crystal chandelier and Nana statue by Niki de Saint-Phalle. Salon Versailles has an ornate coffered ceiling and enormous marble fireplace. The wood-panelled bar has retained its 1913 decor.

### THE BASICS

www.hotel-negresco-nice.com

✚ E7

✉ 37 Promenade des Anglais

☎ 04 93 16 64 00

🍴 Brasserie La Rotonde, Chantecler (▷ 54)

🚍 11, 52, 59, 60, 62, 94, 98

♿ Very good

# Musée des Beaux-Arts

TOP 25

**In a beautiful mansion built for a Ukrainian princess, Nice's museum of fine arts contains an extremely varied collection.**

**Launched by Napoleon III** Nice's original fine arts museum was assembled around the state treasures sent here by Napoleon III after the city became part of France in 1860. Many later bequests have resulted in a collection spanning the 13th to 20th centuries. In 1928 it was moved to this magnificent villa, built for Princess Kotschoubey in 1878.

**Native artists** The museum's official name is the Musée des Beaux-Arts Jules Chéret, after a large donation of works by the creator of modern poster art, who spent his last years in Nice. His

*The Musée des Beaux-Arts is housed in a 19th-century villa that once belonged to Princess Kotschoubey of the Ukraine*

large-scale pastels of women, *The Yellow Domino* and *Lunch on the Grass*, dominate the upper hall. Works by Nice-born Carle Vanloo, principal painter to King Louis XV, are given pride of place on the ground floor. Other highlights of the ground floor rooms include an altarpiece by Ludovic Bréa, *Allegories of the Water and of the Earth* by Jan Brueghel and Hendrick Van Balen, and Jean Honoré Fragonard's *Head of an Ancient*. The upper floor is dedicated to art of the mid-19th to early 20th centuries. There are three sculptures by Rodin, including *The Kiss*. Impressionist and post-Impressionist works include paintings by Monet, Sisley, Bonnard and Vuillard. Raoul Dufy married a girl from Nice and many of his paintings depict scenes from the French Riviera. A large range, from his early fauvist and cubist paintings to mature works, are on display.

## THE BASICS

www.musee-beaux-arts nice.org

➕ C7

✉ 33 avenue des Baumettes

☎ 04 92 15 28 28

🕐 Tue–Sun 10–6; closed 1 Jan, Easter Sunday, 1 May, Christmas

🍴 Few

🚌 3, 8, 9, 10, 12, 22, 23, 38

♿ None

👆 Moderate

PROMENADE DES ANGLAIS TOP 25

# Promenade des Anglais

## HIGHLIGHTS

● Hôtel Negresco (▷ 44–45)
● Sweeping sea views
● Lively atmosphere
● Chairs and arcades to rest in between strolling

## TIP

● Anyone can use the private beaches along the Prom, but you will pay €12–€20 for a sunbed and umbrella. You can eat at the restaurants without using the beach. Free public beaches lie in between, but these have no sunbeds or facilities.

**If you arrived at Nice airport with a good pair of walking shoes, you could stroll into town along the Promenade des Anglais and have a suntan by the time you reached the heart of the city.**

**Seafront path** Built by English visitors in the early 19th century, the Promenade des Anglais curves along the Baie des Anges for around 6km (4 miles), from the old town to the airport. The Reverend Lewis Way paid for its construction out of his own pocket. The project helped local workers who had fallen on hard times during the harsh winter of 1820–21. Local people quickly named it Chemin des Anglais (Path of the English). At first it was only a path just 2m (6.5ft) wide. Gradually palms were planted. It was widened to its present width during the Roaring '20s, and a central strip

*Clockwise from left: a table set for lunch at the beachside Le Meridien restaurant; strolling down the Promenade; enjoying the view over the Baie des Anges; in-line skating—the trendy way to experience the Promenade; the view over Castel Plage*

filled with flowers and palms now separates lanes of busy traffic. In 1931, the Promenade des Anglais was inaugurated by the Duke of Connaught, a son of Queen Victoria.

**The Prom** The broad seaside promenade, filled with strollers, joggers, buskers, cyclists and rollerbladers, overlooks a succession of public and private beaches. The city side is an architectural parade of elegant façades, from belle-époque hotels such as Hôtel Negresco (▷ 44–45) to modern apartment buildings to art deco landmarks like the Palais de la Méditerranée. Completed in 1929 for the American millionaire Frank Jay Gould, this lavish hotel was the scene of extravagant dinners, but it was destroyed by fire in 1934. The façade was restored and a new hotel (▷ 112) and casino built behind in the empty shell.

**THE BASICS**

✚ D8

🍽 Cafes, restaurants

🚍 52, 59, 60, 62, 94, 98, 99

♿ Good

# More to See

### MUSÉE DES ARTS ASIATIQUES

www.arts-asiatiques.com

Kenzo Tange's striking white-marble building of geometric shapes sits by a peaceful lake. The Asian Arts Museum displays a small but superb collection from China, Japan, India and Southeast Asia. A footbridge leads to the teahouse, where Japanese tea ceremonies are sometimes held.

➕ Off map at A9 ✉ 405 Promenade des Anglais, at Parc Phoenix ☎ 04 92 29 37 00 🕐 May to mid-Oct Wed–Mon 10–6; mid-Oct to end Apr Wed–Mon 10–5 🍴 Tea room 🚌 9, 10, 23 ♿ Excellent 🖐 Moderate

### MUSÉE INTERNATIONAL D'ART NAÏF ANATOLY JAKOVSKY

The International Museum of Naïve Art displays some 600 paintings, drawings and other works from the 18th century to the present, based on the collection of the art critic Anatoly Jakovsky. It is housed in the pretty pink Château Sainte-Hélène.

➕ A9 ✉ Avenue de Fabron ☎ 04 93 71 78 33 🕐 Wed–Mon 10–6 🚌 8, 9, 10, 12, 23, 24, 34 ♿ Few 🖐 Moderate

### PALAIS MASSÉNA

Scheduled to reopen in 2008 after a lengthy renovation, this handsome villa now houses Nice's Museum of Art and History. Among the exhibits are local and European paintings, armour, costumes and porcelain, and rooms dedicated to Napoléon, Garibaldi and Marshal Masséna.

➕ E7 ✉ 35 Promenade des Anglais ☎ 04 93 88 11 34 🕐 Call for opening times 🚌 11, 52, 59, 60, 62, 94, 98 🖐 Moderate

### PARC PHOENIX

Covering 7ha (17 acres), Parc Phoenix has one of the largest glasshouses in Europe, with seven different tropical climates and thousands of plant species, from tree ferns to rare orchids. Tropical fish, iguanas, raptors and exotic birds inhabit the botanical gardens, and there is a children's playground too.

➕ Off map at A9 ✉ 405 Promenade des Anglais, opposite the airport ☎ 04 92 29 77 00 🕐 Apr–end Sep daily 9.30–7.30; Oct–end Mar daily 9.30–6 🍴 Café 🚌 9, 10, 23 ♿ Very good 🖐 Inexpensive

*Fountains in the Parc Phoenix*

*The Musée des Arts Asiatiques*

# Famous Promenade

This stroll takes you along Nice's famous Promenade des Anglais. Blue chairs under the arcades let you pause and admire the views.

**DISTANCE:** 0.6km (1 mile) **ALLOW:** 1 hour

**START**

**JARDIN ALBERT I** (▷ 62)
G7 🚌 52, 59, 60, 62, 94, 98, 99

**END**

**MUSÉE DES BEAUX-ARTS** (▷ 46–47)
C7 🚌 3, 8, 9, 10, 12, 22, 23, 38

**1** Start by the carousel in Jardin Albert I. Walk west along the park to admire the Centenary Monument, crowned by a statue of Nikaïa, goddess of victory.

**2** Cross the road at the traffic lights to the seafront side of the Promenade, for better views of the sea and the buildings opposite. Le Meridien Hotel and its Casino Ruhl (▷ 53) have the enviable address '1 Promenade des Anglais'.

**3** Beyond the tourist office (No. 5) is the spectacular art deco façade of the Palais de la Méditerranée at No. 13, all that remains from the extravagant pleasure palace of the interwar years.

**4** Some of the finest buildings on the Promenade lie just beyond: Le Royal hotel (No. 21–23), the Hôtel Westminster Concorde (No. 27), Villa Prat (No. 30) and the neoclassical Hôtel Le West-End next door.

**8** Follow signs on rue de France for the Musée des Beaux-Arts, reached by a left turn on rue Renoir.

**7** Farther along, cross to the other side of the Promenade by Square G. Férrie, where the pretty Palais de l'Agriculture is being restored. Walk along the east side of the square, cross over rue de France, and turn right.

**6** Continue west past several beaches. Opposite Forum Plage are the palm gardens (private) of Villa Furtado Heine (No. 61), built in 1787. At No. 65 is the Centre Universitaire Méditerranéen.

**5** Palais Masséna (▷ 50) is set back from the road in lush gardens, overlooked by the dome of Hôtel Negresco (▷ 44–45). Take a break and admire it from beneath the Promenade arcade.

# Shopping

### ANNE FONTAINE
Fashion designer Anne Fontaine has a smart Nice store where you can find items like her white shirts with a subtle touch of colour.

F7 ⊠ 4 avenue de Suède
☎ 04 93 16 96 25 🚍 Any on the Promenade des Anglais

### AUGUSTIN LATOUR
This lovely shop sells furniture and decorative items from contemporary designers.

F7 ⊠ 6 rue Dalpozzo
☎ 04 93 82 29 02 🚍 3, 8 and others

### BOUTIQUE LACOSTE
www.lacoste.com
Just back from the Promenade des Anglais, off the Jardin Albert I, is a branch of this French clothing company.

F7 ⊠ 6 avenue de Suède
☎ 04 93 87 75 45 🚍 Any on the Promenade des Anglais

### CHANEL
www.chanel.com
Chanel now extends from fashion and fragrances to watches, jewellery and eyewear.

F7 ⊠ 6 rue Paradis
☎ 04 93 88 39 99 🚍 Any bus on Promenade des Anglais

### CLAUDE BONUCCI
www.claude-bonucci.com
French designer Claude Bonucci creates chic and stylish men's clothes that are sure to impress.

F7 ⊠ 10 rue Massenet
☎ 04 93 87 48 87 🚍 Any on the Promenade des Anglais

### EMPORIO ARMANI
www.emporioarmani.com
The place to go for stylish men's fashions.

F7 ⊠ 1 rue Paradis
☎ 04 93 16 16 07 🚍 Any bus on Promenade des Anglais

### ESPACE HARROCH
A concept store covering four floors, with fashions from new designers as well as top names. There's also a home decor area, a tea room and restaurant.

F7 ⊠ 7 rue Paradis
☎ 04 93 82 50 23 🚍 Any bus on Promenade des Anglais

### FAÇONNABLE
Sometimes referred to as the European 'Ralph Lauren', this sportswear brand began in Nice in 1961 and achieved worldwide fame for its fine fabrics and expert tailoring. It is now owned by American department-store chain Nordstrom.

F7 ⊠ 10 rue Paradis
☎ 04 93 88 06 97 🚍 Any bus on Promenade des Anglais

### DESIGNER NAMES
Although there are virtually no shops on the Promenade des Anglais itself, except hotel gift shops, it's not surprising that leading designers want to be seen in the streets just behind. Rue Paradis is home to some of the biggest names in fashion, such as Chanel, Armani, Max Mara and Louis Vuitton.

### HÔTEL NEGRESCO
www.hotel-negresco-nice.com
If you're passing by the Hôtel Negresco, call in to look in their gift shops. There's an exceptionally good collection of jewellery, clothing, accessories and *objets d'art*.

E7 ⊠ 37 Promenade des Anglais ☎ 04 93 16 64 00
🚍 Any bus on the Promenade des Anglais

### LOUIS VUITTON
www.louisvuitton.com
The luxury French luggage and clothing stores go back to 1854, but here, just back from the Promenade des Anglais, you can buy their most up-to-date designs.

F7 ⊠ 2 avenue de Suède
☎ 04 93 87 87 47 🚍 Any on the Promenade des Anglais

### LES NÉRÉÏDES
This shop has a wide selection of jewellery inspired by everything from baroque to ethnic styles, from precious metals to semi-precious stones.

F7 ⊠ 1 rue Paradis
☎ 04 93 82 18 00 🚍 Any on Promenade des Anglais

### SONIA RYKIEL
See the latest fashions from this top designer of women's knitwear, who is known for initiating trendy touches such as fun fur and inside-out sweater seams.

F7 ⊠ 3 rue Paradis
☎ 04 93 87 82 87 🚍 Any on the Promenade des Anglais

# Entertainment and Nightlife

## CASINO RUHL

Choose from more than 300 slot machines, various gaming rooms, roulette, blackjack and poker. The Ruhl also has two restaurants and weekend floor shows with dinner included.

🏠 G7 ✉ 1 Promenade des Anglais ☎ 04 97 03 12 51 ◷ Daily 10am–dawn 🚌 11, 52, 59, 60, 62, 94, 98

## L'ÉVÈNEMENT

www.evenement-club.com
Right on the seafront, l'Évènement is one of the biggest and best night-clubs in Nice, with go-go dancers, DJs and some special events evenings (these have to be booked in advance, so always check ahead). Note that it opens only on weekends and public holidays.

🏠 G7 ✉ 45 Promenade des Anglais ☎ 04 93 96 68 00 ◷ Fri–Sun and public hols; opening times vary, closes 5am 🚌 11, 52, 59, 60, 62, 94, 98

## LA HAVANE

www.lahavanenice.com
Sitting just behind the Promenade des Anglais is this Cuban dance hall/bar/restaurant that's very popular with the locals, who love the nightly live Latin music. The pina coladas flow more freely as the night wears on.

🏠 F7 ✉ 32 rue de France ☎ 04 93 16 36 16 ◷ Daily 4pm–2.30am 🚌 11, 52, 59, 60, 62, 94, 98

## PALAIS DE LA MÉDITERRANÉE

www.lepalaisdela
mediterranee.com
The casino at the revamped Palais de la Méditerranée has become a place to be seen in, with its stylish 1930s art deco look. As well as its extensive gaming facilities it has a restaurant and a theatre with dinner and floor show.

🏠 F7 ✉ 15 Promenade des Anglais ☎ 04 92 14 77 20 ◷ Daily 8pm–dawn 🚌 11, 52, 59, 60, 62, 94, 98

## PALAIS NIKAÏA

www.nikaia.fr
The 'big sea bird' (or so its design suggests) combines a sports arena with a concert hall that stages classical and rock concerts. Although it's a little out of the heart of the city and you might need a taxi, it's quite a venue, so

it's worth checking to see what's on.

🏠 Off map at A9 ✉ 163 route de Grenoble ☎ 04 92 29 31 26 ◷ Box office Mon–Fri 1–6pm 🚌 9, 10, 95 🚉 Nice St-Augustin

## LE RELAIS

www.hotel-negresco-nice.com
One way to get an idea of the Negresco's style if you're not actually staying there is to have a drink in the Relais Bar. The bar was designed in an English style in honour of the creators of the Promenade des Anglais and its rich decor of wal-nut wood panelling and tapestries hasn't changed since the hotel opened in 1913. There's a piano player every evening except Mondays, and a special monthly cocktail created by the bar team, along with a large choice of single malt whiskies and Caribbean rums.

🏠 E7 ✉ Hôtel Negresco, 37 Promenade des Anglais ☎ 04 93 16 64 00 ◷ 11.30am–midnight (until 1am in summer) 🚌 11, 52, 59, 60, 62, 94, 98

## RIALTO

Just back from the Promenade des Anglais is this cinema showing the latest films in their original language, with French subtitles.

🏠 E7 ✉ 4 rue de Rivoli ☎ 08 36 68 00 41 ◷ Daily 🚌 11, 52, 59, 60, 62, 94, 98

# Restaurants

## BEAU RIVAGE PLAGE (€€)

The beachside summer restaurant of the Beau Rivage hotel is a popular spot on a sunny day. Much of the menu comes right out of the sea, such as the *trinitée des poissons* (dourade, sardines and gambas) with ratatouille.

➕ G7 ✉ 107 quai des États-Unis ☎ 04 92 47 82 82 🕐 May–end Oct daily lunch, dinner 🚌 Any bus along Promenade des Anglais

## BLEU CITRON (€€€)

www.radissonsas.com
The blue and lemon decor that gives the Bleu Citron its name lends a cheerful Mediterranean feel to the Radisson's star restaurant, which suits the imaginative cooking.

➕ B9 ✉ Hôtel Radisson SAS, 223 Promenade des Anglais ☎ 04 97 17 71 77 🕐 Daily lunch, dinner 🚌 Any bus along Promenade des Anglais

## BRASSERIE LA ROTONDE (€€)

www.hotel-negresco-nice.com
The Negresco's more casual restaurant is a cheerful place, with fairground decoration and carousel horses. There's nothing casual about the food, though, which comes from the same kitchen as the Michelin-starred Chantecler (▷ this page). Enjoy a salad or sandwich, or something more elaborate, such as a whole sea bass grilled with dried fennel and aniseed butter.

➕ E7 ✉ Hôtel Negresco, 37 Promenade des Anglais ☎ 04 93 16 64 00 🕐 Daily 7am–11.30pm 🚌 Any bus along Promenade des Anglais

## LA CANNE À SUCRE (€–€€)

This place stands out for its good food and friendly service. Local dishes such as daube and home-made pizzas are popular, and there's also a piano bar around the corner if you want to enjoy an after-dinner drink.

➕ F7 ✉ 11 Promenade des Anglais ☎ 04 93 87 19 35 🕐 Daily 8am–10pm 🚌 Any along Promenade des Anglais

## LE CAPRICE (€€€)

www.starwoodhotels.com
The Sheraton's Caprice restaurant serves superb French/Mediterranean dishes, but it closes in summer, when service switches to the swimming-pool terrace.

➕ D8 ✉ Four Points by Sheraton Hotel, 59 Promenade des Anglais ☎ 04 93 97 90 90 🕐 Oct–end May daily lunch, dinner 🚌 Any bus along Promenade des Anglais

## CHANTECLER (€€€)

www.hotel-negresco-nice.com
With its setting inside the Hôtel Negresco, and its Michelin-star rating, this is one of Nice's great—and most expensive—dining experiences. Dishes can be deliciously simple, like the soft-boiled egg on toast with Iranian caviar.

➕ E7 ✉ Hôtel Negresco, 37 Promenade des Anglais ☎ 04 93 16 64 00 🕐 Daily lunch, dinner 🚌 Any bus along Promenade des Anglais

## LES JARDINS DU CAPITOLE (€€)

If you want to dine with a view of the Baie des Anges then this is the place. Unusually for Nice, the menu is more meat-based than seafood.

➕ D8 ✉ 52 Promenade des Anglais ☎ 04 93 44 78 81 🕐 Daily lunch, dinner 🚌 Any along Promenade des Anglais

Central Nice

**Central Nice has handsome art nouveau buildings, smart restaurants and museums of modern art and photography. Place Masséna, with its geyser-like fountain, leads to the city's main shopping streets.**

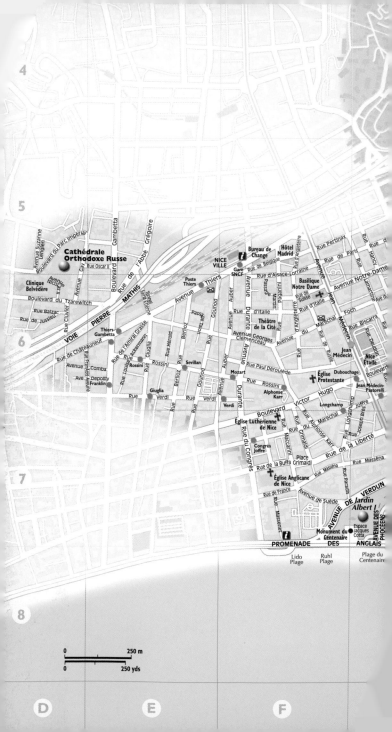

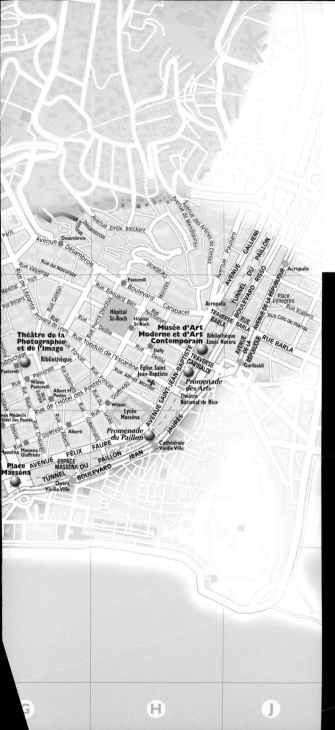

Central Nice

# Cathédrale Orthodoxe Russe

*The colourful exterior of the Russian Orthodox Cathedral*

## THE BASICS

🚻 D5
✉ Avenue Nicolas II
🕐 May–end Sep daily 9–noon, 2.30–6; Oct, mid-Feb to end Apr daily 9.15–noon, 2.30–5.30; Nov to mid-Feb daily 9.30–noon, 2.30–5
🚌 4, 7, 64, 75
♿ Few
💰 Inexpensive
❓ Sunday service 10am, lasts 2 hours; congregation stands throughout

## HIGHLIGHTS

● Ornate façade
● Icon of St. Nicholas
● Icon of the Virgin of Kazan
● Iconostasis
● Enamelled bronze casket representing Christ lying in the Holy Sepulchre

**The whimsical nature of the colourful spires and shiny onion domes does little to prepare you for the peacefulness inside. Take time to reflect amid the tranquil beauty.**

**Russian gem** There's no finer symbol of the Russian expat community that settled in Nice in the 19th century than this stunning Orthodox cathedral. Built between 1903 and 1912, it was the first Russian Orthodox church outside Russia to be designated with cathedral status. It was erected in memory of the tzarevich Nicolas Alexandrovich, heir to the Russian throne, who died in Nice in 1865 aged 21, in a villa that once stood in the cathedral grounds. The façade replicates the style of Moscow churches at the turn of the 18th century, with two porch entries, a tall central cupola surrounded by four smaller cupolas and a bell tower, all ornately carved and decorated with gleaming tiles.

**Peaceful beauty** Though no less lavish, the spacious interior has a tranquil, reflective atmosphere intended to symbolise the beauty and purity of the cosmos. Pick up an information sheet at the entrance, which explains the meaning and origin of the beautiful iconostasis and the many icons. On the left of the sanctuary is a mysterious icon of St. Nicholas that belonged to the tzarevich. It hung outside his mortuary chapel for 20 years, turning black in the sun, but recovered its original state when brought into the cathedral. To the right is the much-venerated icon of the Virgin of Kazan, adorned with semi-precious stones.

*A façade on Place Masséna (left); relaxing in Espace Masséna (right)*

TOP 25

# Place Masséna

**A new tramline has sparked a handsome renewal of Nice's biggest pedestrian square. Catch an outdoor concert here and you'll see why it's the heart of the city's social life.**

**An elegant bridge** Nice's beautiful central square, which bridges the River Paillon, acquired its current form in the 1830s, when the north side was built in a unified, neoclassical style. Lined with elegant arcades and shuttered buildings with bright coats of Sardinian red, it's a city landmark. The square is named after Maréchal André Masséna, a native of Nice, who fought under Napoléon to defend France from Russian and Austrian invasions in the late 18th century. By 1900 it was criss-crossed with tramlines, but in the latter 20th century it became clogged with traffic. In 2007 Place Masséna was transformed into a pedestrian-only space, with a chequerboard surface and a new tramline.

**Fountains and flowers** At the square's southern end is the fabulous Fontaine du Soleil (Fountain of the Sun), installed in 1956. The five bronze groups by Alfred Janniot represent the planets of the solar system. The watery plumes shoot geyser-like into the sky. Broad, balustrade-lined steps nearby lead down to the old town. Place Masséna anchors the lower end of the Promenade du Paillon (▷ 62). On the east side, more fountains, flowers and benches fill Espace Masséna, a peaceful spot with lovely views of the distant hills. West is the lush Jardin Albert I (▷ 62). Nice's main shopping street, avenue Jean Médecin, runs north from the square.

**THE BASICS**

G7

None on the square but plenty nearby

Many, including 1, 2, 4, 8, 15, 52, 59, 94

**HIGHLIGHTS**

- Fontaine du Soleil
- Handsome architecture
- Espace Masséna

# Musée d'Art Moderne et d'Art Contemporain

## HIGHLIGHTS

- The Esplanade
- Salle Niki de Saint-Phalle
- Salle Yves Klein
- Salle Nouveau Realisme–
Pop Art

## TIP

- The 235-seat Jean-Étienne Marie Auditorium is used for lectures and seminars with art critics and other art specialists. These are open to the public. Small concerts and chamber music recitals are also held here.

**Just beyond place Garibaldi at the edge of the Vieille Ville, this striking marble building houses major avant-garde art and is itself a monument to modern art.**

Cutting edge art All the main avant-garde movements from the 1960s onwards are given a showcase in the Museum of Modern Art and Contemporary Art, often known simply as MAMAC. A rotating display of exhibits from the permanent collection includes works by French and American artists, particularly the French New Realists, the Nice School and American Pop Art. The impressive building, whose four massive towers are linked by glass-walled walkways, opened in 1990. Its spacious rooms do justice to the often-monumental works of art. The above-ground Esplanade runs between the museum and the Théâtre National

*Even the building is a work of art at the Musée d'Art Moderne et d'Art Contemporain*

de Nice, with wonderful views and sculptures by Niki de Saint-Phalle, Alexander Calder and others.

**Artists on show** Temporary exhibitions are held on the first floor and contemporary gallery, while the upper floors display works from the permanent collection. On the second floor, some of the 190 works donated by Niki de Saint-Phalle are displayed in a large room alongside works by her close associate Jean Tinguely. Another room is dedicated to the art of Nice-born Yves Klein, with many of his 'blue' paintings. Also here are works by Christo, César, Lichtenstein, Oldenburg and Warhol. The third floor looks at American Abstraction through such artists as Frank Stella and Kenneth Noland, and artists of the Nice School, particularly the Fluxus movement active here between 1963 and 1973.

**THE BASICS**

www.mamac-nice.org

➕ H6

✉ Promenade des Arts

☎ 04 97 13 42 01

🕐 Tue–Sun 10–6; closed 1 Jan, Easter Sunday, 1 May, Christmas

🍽 Café

🚌 1, 2, 5, 6, 7, 9, 10, 14, 16, 17, 25

♿ Very good

💷 Moderate

# More to See

### JARDIN ALBERT I
Named after the King of Belgium, these lush gardens between Place Masséna and the Promenade des Anglais are the oldest in Nice. Concerts are held in the 19th-century bandstand and the Théâtre de Verdure. On the lawn, the sculpture *L'Arc* by Bernar Venet is 19m (62ft) high.

🚇 G7 🚌 Many, including 1, 2, 4, 8, 15, 52, 59, 60, 62, 94, 98, 99

### PROMENADE DES ARTS
Traverse Barla crosses the old channel of the River Paillon. On the north side is the Acropolis, a massive convention centre. On the south side a string of cultural institutions, known as the Promenade des Arts, was built on the covered riverbed. The Bibliothèque Louis Nucera, the main library, is topped by the beautiful terraced gardens of Jardin Maréchal Juin. Among its sculptures is the monumental *Tête Carrée* (*Square Head*) by Sosno, 30m (98ft) high. Paths lead uphill through the gardens to the Musée d'Art Moderne et d'Art Contemporain

(▷ 60–61). The promenade ends at the Théâtre National de Nice.

🚇 H6 🕐 Jardin Maréchal Juin: Jun–end Aug Tue–Sun 10–8; Apr, May, Sep, Oct Tue–Sun 10–7; Nov–end Mar Tue–Sun 10–6

🚌 30, 25, 17, 3, 5, 6, 17 🦽 Good 🎫 Free

### PROMENADE DU PAILLON
Much of the River Paillon was covered over in the 19th century to prevent it bursting its banks. The Promenade du Paillon runs on top of the riverbed from the Théâtre National de Nice to the sea. The promenade includes a series of delightful gardens: Square Général Le Clerc, Espace Masséna (▷ 59) and Jardin Albert I (▷ this page).

🚇 H7 🚌 98, 1, 2, 11, 5, 6, 17, 14, 25

### THÉÂTRE DE LA PHOTOGRAPHIE ET DE L'IMAGE
www.tpi-nice.org
This impressive photography museum showcases a range of international artists and photographic styles.

🚇 G6 ✉ 27 boulevard Dubouchage 🕾 04 97 13 42 20 🕐 Tue–Sun 10–6 🚌 1, 2, 4, 5, 12, 15, 17, 22 🦽 Few 🎫 Free

*Fountains in front of the Acropolis*

*The Loch Ness Monster, outside the Théâtre National de Nice*

# A Calming Stroll

The gardens and esplanades along the Promenade du Paillon and Promenade des Arts make a pleasant break from the urban bustle.

**DISTANCE:** 1.2km (0.7 miles) **ALLOW:** 1 hour

**START**

**JARDIN MARÉCHAL JUIN** (▷ 62)
➕ H6 🚌 3, 5, 6, 17, 25, 30

**1** Stroll through the Jardin Maréchal Juin above the Bibliothèque Louis Nucera. The terraces are filled with sculptures. There are views of MAMAC, the Acropolis and the *Square Head*.

**2** Walk along avenue St-Jean Baptiste to the Musée d'Art Moderne et d'Art Contemporain (▷ 60–61). Climb the stairs between the tower to reach the esplanade between the museum and the Théâtre National. Admire the sculptures and views.

**3** Return to ground level via the stairs at the theatre end. This marks the end of the Promenade des Arts.

**4** Cross the street and continue straight ahead on avenue Félix Faure, along the pavement beside the bus station. When you reach a staircase climb up to explore the gardens above, which form the top end of the Promenade du Paillon.

**END**

**JARDIN ALBERT I** (▷ 62)
➕ G7 🚌 1, 2, 4, 8, 15, 52, 59 and others

**8** Stroll through Jardin Albert I (▷ 62) to the sea.

**7** Continue into Place Masséna (▷ 59), Nice's beautiful central square.

**6** Cross the street into Espace Masséna (▷ 59) and enjoy its playful fountains.

**5** Return to ground level via the steps beside the car park. Continue straight ahead into pretty Square Général Le Clerc. Walk through here on the paths beneath the iron arches.

# Shopping

## CARTIER
www.cartier.com
The famous French jeweller has a store just off Place Masséna, with the usual array of desirable designer items.
⊞ G7 ⊠ 4 avenue de Verdun ☎ 04 92 14 48 20 🚌 11

## CRÉANOVA
www.creanova.fr
High design, but fun as well, this shop has a great range of creative objects for the home, from cheese graters designed by Philippe Starck to personalized Pop Art photos à la Warhol.
⊞ G7 ⊠ 27 rue Hôtel des Postes ☎ 04 93 62 36 67 🚌 3, 7, 9 and others

## ELIZABETH CONTAL
Gemstones are incorporated with other natural materials into the jewellery of this designer, who also blends perfumes by computer based on the moment of your birth.
⊞ G7 ⊠ 16 rue de la Liberté ☎ 04 93 87 30 37 🚌 3, 7, 9 and others

## ENFANT TI AGE
www.enfant-ti-age.com
One of the things the French do really well is producing fun and yet fashionable items for children. Here it's mostly furniture (you can ship it back home) but there are other accessories too.
⊞ G6 ⊠ 3 rue Gubernatis ☎ 08 73 65 89 79 🚌 11 and others

## LA FERME FROMAGÈRE
This specialist cheese shop runs cheese-tasting sessions on a Thursday and Saturday evenings, and Friday afternoons and evenings. Phone first, as they're subject to change.
⊞ G6 ⊠ 27 rue Lépante ☎ 04 93 62 52 34 🚌 37

## HERMÈS
www.hermes.com
Perfumes and gifts, from the trademark scarves to chic fashions.
⊞ G7 ⊠ 8 avenue de Verdun ☎ 04 93 87 75 03 🚌 11

## KITCHEN BAZAAR
Another of Nice's excellent kitchen shops, with useful utensils and good gift items for any foodies back home.
⊞ G7 ⊠ 20 rue de la Liberté ☎ 04 93 82 01 02 🚌 3, 7, 9 and others

## AVENUE JEAN MÉDECIN
Avenue Jean Médecin is Nice's main shopping street, running from Place Masséna north to avenue Thiers, near the train station. It is lined with all the major French and European high-street names selling low and mid-price fashions, shoes and accessories. It's no wonder that the new tram line was installed along this broad, busy avenue, with a stop right outside Nice's big mall, Nice Étoile.

## LOFT DESIGN
www.loft-design.com
The Nice branch (there's one other, in Lille) of a designer specializing in furniture and other household objects.
⊞ F7 ⊠ 25 rue de la Buffa ☎ 04 93 16 09 09 🚌 8 and others

## MAX MARA
Elegantly stylish ready-to-wear clothing from the house of Max Mara, founded by Italian designer Achille Maramotti.
⊞ G7 ⊠ 22 rue de la Liberté ☎ 04 93 16 05 15 🚌 3, 7, 9 and others

## NICE ÉTOILE
www.nicetoile.com
The largest shopping mall in the heart of the city, Nice Étoile has 100 boutiques selling jewellery, fashion, shoes, bags and many other items. There is also a branch of C&A.
⊞ G6 ⊠ 30 avenue Jean-Médecin ☎ 04 92 17 38 17 🚌 1, 2 or any bus along avenue Jean-Médecin

## LE PAPIER
Stationery is an everyday item that the French turn into something special, with their quality paper and creative designs. This shop has paper of all shapes and sizes and is a good place to shop for a gift for the writer in the family.
⊞ F6 ⊠ 10 rue de Russie ☎ 04 93 85 17 75 🚌 1, 2 or any bus along avenue Jean-Médecin

# Entertainment and Nightlife

## LE BEFORE
Although it serves some basic food, Le Before is more the kind of atmospheric place that the city's clubbers go to for an early aperitif, to be replaced later by post-dinner drinkers on their late-night cocktails.
⊞ F7 ⊠ 18 rue des Congrès ☎ 04 93 87 85 59 ⓒ Daily 6pm–2am 🚌 217

## LA BODEGUITA DEL HAVANA
There are salsa classes on Wednesdays and Thursdays at this hugely popular Cuban place, with a house salsa band playing nightly and other music styles too, including R&B and reggae.
⊞ G7 ⊠ 14 rue Chauvain ☎ 04 93 92 67 24 ⓒ Tue–Sun 8pm–2.30am (music starts 10pm) 🚌 15 and others

## CAVE ROMAGNAN
www.caveromagnan.com
By day an unassuming mix of bar and café, two nights a week the Cave Romagnan turns into a jumping jazz venue, sometimes with poetry nights, too. On music nights the small room is full to overflowing, mostly with a bohemian bunch of locals who drink and dance the night away. There's a fantastic local atmosphere, rare to find these days.
⊞ F6 ⊠ 22 rue d'Angleterre ☎ 04 93 87 91 55 ⓒ Jazz nights Wed, Sat 8.30–11.30 🚌 12, 30, 4 and others

## CHECK POINT
www.checkpointpub.com
The Check Point calls itself an Irish disco pub because, as well as the usual pub atmosphere and sports screens, there's a DJ and also live music every weekend. There's free WiFi too, and a happy hour from opening time (4pm) to 9pm.
⊞ G7 ⊠ 2 rue Desboutin ☎ 04 93 13 96 92 ⓒ Daily 4pm–2.30am 🚌 All buses to Gare Routière

## CINÉMATHÈQUE DE NICE
www.cinematheque-nice.com
The Cinémathèque is in the Acropolis complex and puts on a variety of movies, from classics to cutting-edge contemporary, shown in their original language.
⊞ J6 ⊠ 3 esplanade Kennedy ☎ 04 92 04 06 66 ⓒ Tue–Sun, film times vary 🚌 3, 5, 6

## KARR BAR
Although this place is a good and smart French restaurant, it also has a separate lounge bar with its own DJ, who attracts

### A NIGHT OUT

Most visitors head for the old town but there are plenty of nightlife options elsewhere in the city, which the locals know and love. Look in hotels and tourist offices for listings magazines (mostly in French), and flyers, too.

a local 30-something crowd for the drinks and music.
⊞ F7 ⊠ 10 rue Alphonse Karr ☎ 04 93 82 18 31 ⓒ Mon–Sat 6.30–11.30pm (restaurant opens 7.30) 🚌 38

## L'ODACE
It doesn't look much from the outside, but inside the Odace has a laid-back Oriental atmosphere in its bar areas, where you can relax before moving on to the dance floors.
⊞ F6 ⊠ 29 rue Alphonse Karr ☎ 04 93 82 37 66 ⓒ Tue–Thu 7pm–2.30am, Fri, Sat 7pm–5am 🚌 38

## LE SANSAS
This large bar just off Place Masséna has a large terrace, sports screens, free WiFi, good cocktails and equally good prices, making it very popular. There's live music some evenings.
⊞ G7 ⊠ 4 avenue des Phocéens ☎ 04 93 85 03 14 ⓒ Wed–Sun 11am–12.30am 🚌 All buses to Gare Routière

## THÉÂTRE NATIONAL DE NICE
www.nice-coteazur.org
The TNN has become one of the major theatres in this part of France, with an eclectic range of productions, from ancient to contemporary drama.
⊞ H6 ⊠ Promenade des Arts ☎ 04 93 13 90 90 ⓒ Box office Tue–Sat 2–7 🚌 All buses to Gare Routière

# Restaurants

## PRICES

Prices are approximate, based on a three-course meal for one person.

| €€€ | over €50 |
|---|---|
| €€ | €20–€50 |
| € | under €20 |

### APHRODITE (€€€)

www.restaurant-aphrodite.com
Some of the best food in Nice is to be had on the flower-filled terrace of Aphrodite, or amid the cool modern lines of its dining room. Sea bass steamed with mushrooms is a signature dish.
🖼 G6 ✉ 10 boulevard Dubouchage ☎ 04 93 85 63 53 🕐 Tue–Sat lunch, dinner 🚌 38

### LA BAIE D'AMALFI (€–€€)

www.baie-amalfi.com
With seating inside and out, the Baie d'Amalfi is a hugely popular place and provides value-for-money menus and specials based on what's in the market. There's a good choice of meat and fish, and the pasta and home-made gnocchi are first rate.
🖼 G7 ✉ 9 rue Gustave Deloye ☎ 04 93 80 01 21 🕐 Daily lunch, dinner; closed Jul 🚌 15 and others

### BRASSERIE FLO NICE (€€)

www.flonice.com
Brasserie Flo is fun. In a 1930s theatre, the kitchen is on stage and it's an apt way to present the drama and flourish that is typical of a French brasserie at its busy best. Book ahead and ask for a good balcony seat. Expect brasserie fare (steak, fresh fish) with a Provençal twist.
🖼 G7 ✉ 2-4 rue Sacha Guitry ☎ 04 93 13 38 38 🕐 Daily lunch, dinner 🚌 15 and others

### LE CENAC (€€)

Bright blue umbrellas shade the tables of this wonderful place, with a pizzeria on one side and a bistro on the other. There's a bar at one end where people call in for a drink and a chat. The food is superb, with dishes such as duck breast in honey or risotto with scallops.
🖼 G6 ✉ 18 rue Biscarra ☎ 04 93 92 46 93 🕐 Mon–Sat lunch, dinner 🚌 1, 2 or any bus along Jean Médecin

### AOC WINE...

Nice is the only city in France with a vineyard that has been given AOC (Appellation d'Origine Contrôlée) status. The AOC system guarantees quality by laying down rules about the kinds of grapes used, growing methods, alcoholic yield and so on. In Nice, the wines of Bellet, one of the oldest wine-growing regions in France, meet these requirements. If you see a bottle on a wine list you should certainly try it.

### LES ÉPICURIENS (€€)

With its terrace on place Wilson and a cosy dining room inside, this is an increasingly popular spot with local gourmets—and if local people rave over its tasting menu of regional dishes then you know it has to be good.
🖼 G6 ✉ 6 place Wilson ☎ 04 93 80 85 00 🕐 Mon–Fri lunch, dinner, Sat dinner; closed Aug 🚌 1, 2, or any bus along Jean Médecin

### INDYANA (€€)

Very chic and popular with a hip young Nice crowd, the Indyana doesn't sacrifice fashion for food. It's also one of the best tables in town. Sea bass baked in salt and carved at the table is the house special.
🖼 G7 ✉ 11 rue Gustave Deloye ☎ 04 93 80 67 69 🕐 Tue–Sat lunch, dinner; Mon, Sun dinner 🚌 15 and others

### KEISUKE MATSUSHIMA (€€€)

www.keisukematsushima.com
This is where a young Japanese chef, who trained in French cuisine in Tokyo, has come to France to cook and has quickly earned himself a Michelin star. He takes Provençal food and gives it the subtle Japanese touch in dishes such as butternut squash in a creamy risotto with truffle and dried parma ham.
🖼 F7 ✉ 22 ter rue de France ☎ 04 93 82 26 06 🕐 Mon dinner, Tue–Sat lunch, dinner 🚌 8 and others

### LOU NISSART (€€)

In a side street off Place Masséna and in sight of the fountain, Lou Nissart has outdoor tables under a canopy and more seating inside. Gnocchi, ravioli and other pasta is made on the premises, and the fish soup makes a marvellous starter.

➕ G7  ✉ 1 rue de l'Opéra
☎ 04 93 85 34 49
🕐 Fri–Wed lunch, dinner; closed Thu  🚌 15 and any bus to Place Masséna

### LUC SALSEDO (€€)

Luc Salsedo has worked with Alain Ducasse at the Louis XV in Monaco, and his cooking has been highly praised for its imaginative flair. By keeping the choices limited he manages to produce a well-priced set menu. There are only 30 covers, so book ahead.

➕ F7  ✉ 14 rue Maccarani
☎ 04 93 82 24 12  🕐 Sep–Jun Fri, Sun–Tue lunch, dinner, Thu, Sat dinner; Jul, Aug Mon–Sat dinner only; closed 3 weeks in Jan  🚌 3, 7, 9 and others

### MIREILLE (€€)

This is a little out of the way in the Italian quarter of Nice, and it makes only one main course dish—authentic Spanish paella. People happily travel across the city to try it, it's that good.

➕ G5  ✉ 19 boulevard Raimbaldi  ☎ 04 93 85 27 23
🕐 Wed–Sun lunch, dinner; closed some weeks in Jan, Jun and Aug  🚌 30 and others

### LA PART DES ANGES (€€)

A very special eating (and drinking) experience is to be had at the Angel's Share, a wine cellar with just a few tables. The owner makes you feel at home and enthusiastically recommends wines from his vast collection to accompany the impressively cooked dishes, such as crayfish tails with Parmesan shavings.

➕ G6  ✉ 17 rue Gubernatis
☎ 04 93 62 69 80  🕐 Mon–Thu noon–8, Fri, Sat lunch, dinner  🚌 4 and others

### LA PETITE BICHE (€)

Locals pour in here as soon as it opens, and there's soon a boisterous atmosphere as people tuck into the simple fixed-price menu. There are four main courses to choose from.

➕ F5  ✉ 9 rue Alsace-Lorraine  ☎ 04 93 87 30 70
🕐 Daily lunch, dinner  🚌 12 and others

### ...AND OLIVE OIL

Nice also has an AOC for its olive oil. If you see the name 'Olive de Nice' it means that olives from the local *cailletier* tree have been used and are sold as olives, olive oil or olive purée. The AOC status was granted in 2001 and has seen sales improve to the extent that there are now 400,000 olive trees in the AOC region.

### RESTAURANT BOCCACCIO (€€€)

www.boccaccio-nice.com
Boccaccio is very popular and well-regarded for what you might call Mediterranean Rim cuisine—bouillabaisse from Marseille, paella from Valencia and, of course, locally caught fresh fish.

➕ G7  ✉ 7 rue Masséna
☎ 04 93 87 71 76  🕐 Daily lunch, dinner  🚌 15 and others

### RESTAURANT STÉPHANE VIANO (€€)

Chef Stéphane Viano made the Don Camillo a great success and he has now started his own restaurant, which is equally recommended. His menu focuses on contemporary versions of traditional Nice dishes.

➕ F7  ✉ 26 boulevard Victor Hugo  ☎ 04 93 82 48 63
🕐 Mon–Sat lunch, dinner
🚌 3, 7, 9 and others

### L'UNIVERS DE CHRISTIAN PLUMAIL (€€€)

www.christian-plumail.com
Christian Plumail is one of the top chefs in Nice and his contemporary take on dishes using local ingredients has earned him a Michelin star. His tasting menu, based on what's fresh in the markets, is highly recommended. Book ahead.

➕ H7  ✉ 54 boulevard Jean Jaurès  ☎ 04 93 62 32 22
🕐 Tue–Fri lunch, dinner; Mon, Sat dinner  🚌 All buses to Gare Routière

Cimiez has been a fashionable residential area since the end of the 18th century. Today, among the handsome homes and grand hotels, are art museums, a monastery and Roman remains.

| Sights | 72–78 |
|---|---|

Pré Catélan

Avenue Michel de Cimiez

Voie Romaine

Avenue du Monastère

**Cimitière du Monastère de Cimiez**

*Parc et Jardin des Arènes de Cimiez*

rènes e Cimiez

Rue Joseph Gazan

Montée Barelli

**Monastère Franciscain de Cimiez**

**Musée Henri Matisse**

Corniche Frère Marc

Pasteur

Avenue du Maréchal Lyautey

enue Monte-Croce

Ave Bellanda

enue Salonina

Corniche Frère Marc

Boulevard

Pont Vincent Auriol

Avenue

Le Paillon Torr

Avenue du Maréchal Lyautey

Risso

ia

Corniche Sainte-Rosalie

Che Sainte-Rosalie

Rue Curie

Pasteur

Boulevard

Ave de l'Arbre inférieur

Ruelle de l'Eau Fraîche

Rue de la Gendarmerie

Avenue Ratti

Avenue Ratti

Avenue de Savoie

Provence

Avenue de l'Arbre Inférieur

MALRAUX

Rue El Nouzah

H　　　J　　　K

## HIGHLIGHTS

● *Portrait of Madame Matisse*, 1905
● Le Bleu Matisse room
● The sculpture collection
● Photographs of Matisse at work
● Chairs and tables that feature in Matisse's paintings

**See Matisse's sculptures, drawings and early works, along with photographs, furniture and personal possessions, and get a broader picture of this popular artist, who made Nice his home.**

**Adopted son** Born in 1869, Henri Matisse moved to Paris as a young man, where he took up painting at the age of 20. He became a leading painter of the fauvist movement, and was best known for his colourful, expressive paintings. In 1917 he came to Nice to recuperate from bronchitis, and was so taken with the clarity of the light that he made Nice his home for most of the rest of his life. He spent his final years in Cimiez, where he bought two apartments in the Hôtel Régina. He died in 1954 and is buried in the Cimiez cemetery, next to the monastery church.

*The Matisse Museum is in a 17th-century villa with Provençal shutters and trompe-l'oeil window frames. It displays works from all periods of the artist's life*

**A lifetime's work** The museum occupies a 17th-century Genoese-style villa, painted bright red, with trompe-l'oeil balconies and window frames. It stands in an olive grove in the Parc des Arènes, opposite Matisse's last home in the Hôtel Régina. The collection covers all periods of Matisse's life, from his first paintings in 1890 to key works from his fauvist period to the large-scale mural cut-outs of 1953. It includes an important collection of 57 sculptures, as well as numerous drawings, engravings and studies for the decoration of the chapel at Vence (▷ 99). Matisse's favourite possessions are also on display, many of which, like the *fauteuil rocaille* (armchair), featured in his paintings. Don't miss the wonderful collection of photographs of Matisse, his family and friends, displayed above the atrium. They were taken by famous photographers such as Henri Cartier-Bresson.

## THE BASICS

www.musee-matisse-nice.org

✚ H2

✉ 164 avenue des Arènes

☎ 04 93 81 08 08

🕐 Apr–end Sep Wed–Mon 10–6; Oct–end Mar Wed–Mon 10–5; closed 1 Jan, Easter Sun, 1 May, 25 Dec

🍴 None

🚌 15, 17, 20, 22, 25

♿ Good

💷 Moderate

# Musée Marc Chagall

## HIGHLIGHTS

● The Biblical Message cycle
● Stained-glass windows in the concert hall
● The mosaic of Elijah reflected in a pool

## TIP

● Don't miss the exquisite stained-glass windows in the concert hall, with their beautiful deep blue, violet and mauve hues. These are some of the finest windows Chagall ever conceived, and this is a rare chance to examine his technique close-up.

**Even if you're not religious, Chagall's large-scale renditions of these Biblical stories are impressive. The stunning stained-glass windows in the concert hall are some of his finest creations.**

**Artistic roots** Marc Chagall was born in Belarus in 1887 into a large Jewish family. After studying art in St. Petersburg, he went to Paris in 1910. During his early career he moved between Paris and Russia until becoming a French citizen in 1937. During World War II he escaped the Nazi occupation and fled to the US, returning in 1946. Drawn to Provence, he spent the last 20 years of his life in St-Paul-de-Vence, where he died in 1985, aged 97.

**The Biblical Message** From early childhood, Chagall was fascinated by the stories of the Bible.

*Clockwise from left: the museum's striking entrance; the Mediterranean gardens; art by Marc Chagall; detail of a mosaic*

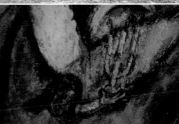

His paintings convey his view of it as a symbol for Nature. In 1930 the art dealer Ambroise Vollard asked Chagall to illustrate a Bible. Deeply moved on a trip to the Holy Land, he was inspired to begin work on the Old Testament scenes that would later form the Biblical Message paintings. These 17 large-scale paintings were created between 1954 and 1967. The stories of Adam and Eve, Noah's Ark, Moses and others are portrayed with vivid colour and movement, using many of Chagall's characteristic symbols.

**Rich donation** The paintings held great meaning for Chagall and he wanted them to remain in his adopted country. He donated them for the creation of this museum, along with preparatory sketches, early gouaches, drawings, etchings, lithographs and sculptures.

## THE BASICS

www.musee-chagall.fr
✚ G4
✉ Avenue Dr. Ménard
☎ 04 93 53 87 20
🕐 Jul–end Sep Wed–Mon 10–6; Oct–end Jun Wed–Mon 10–5; closed 1 Jan, 1 May, 25 Dec
🍽 None
🚌 15
♿ Very good
💷 Moderate

# Parc des Arènes de Cimiez

| HIGHLIGHTS |
| --- |

- The amphitheatre
- The North Bath
- Bronze figures
- Games of the Ancients

| TIP |
| --- |

- The museums in the Parc des Arènes do not have cafés and there are none in the surrounding residential district. The only option for refreshments is the snack bar in the park, which serves salads, pizza and light fare.

**It's exciting to find these Roman ruins so well preserved in the middle of a busy city, but today's residents don't keep them under wraps: the ancient amphitheatre is a venue for the Nice Jazz Festival.**

**Roman Nice** Cimiez stands on the site of the Roman settlement of Cemenelum, founded in 14BC. The thriving city had some 20,000 residents and was the capital of the Alpes Maritimae province until it was destroyed by barbarian invasions in the 4th century. Remains of this Gallo-Roman city have been excavated in the southern portion of the Parc des Arènes de Cimiez. The small amphitheatre, Les Arènes, has many original arches intact and stands outside the archaeology museum. Behind the museum are the remains of the public baths, where you can see remnants

*Learn more about life in Roman times at the Parc des Arènes de Cimiez*

of the hypocaust heating and water flow systems. The North Bath (Thermes du Nord), with its high walls, is the best preserved. The red façade of the Matisse Museum in the background makes a striking contrast. There is also a residential district with ancient streets and shop foundations.

**Musée Archéologique** The archaeology museum has an extensive collection of items from Cemenelum and the surrounding region. Among the fascinating finds are ceramics, glasswork and bronze objects such as the Masque de Silène and a large figure of a boar. Displays of practical and decorative objects portray life in Gallo-Roman times, from a model kitchen to the necropolis on the lower level. Be sure to see the 'Games of the Ancients' section, where you can try your hand at *osselets*, dice and ancient board games.

## THE BASICS

www.musee-archeologique-nice.org

➕ H2

✉ 160 avenue des Arènes

☎ 04 93 81 59 57

🕐 Wed–Mon 10–6; closed 1 Jan, Easter Sun, 1 May, 25 Dec

🍴 None

🚌 15, 17, 20, 22

♿ Few

✋ Moderate

# More to See

### CIMETIÈRE DU MONASTÈRE DE CIMIEZ

Two of Nice's greatest artists are buried in this cemetery beside the monastery church, which is full of elaborate tombs. Henri Matisse rests beneath a simple stone slab in a peaceful spot in the shade of an olive tree, apart from the main graveyard; follow signs to the left as you enter. At the opposite end behind the church is the grave of Raoul Dufy, surrounded by a half-circle of small pines.

✚ J2 ✉ Avenue des Arènes ⏰ Daily 8–6
🚌 15, 17, 20, 22 ♿ None ✋ Free

### JARDIN DES ARÈNES DE CIMIEZ

North of the archaeological sites, the Parc des Arènes de Cimiez is covered by a beautiful olive grove, whose winding paths are named after jazz musicians. The Nice Jazz Festival and other major festivals take place here. Concerts are held in the bandstand.

✚ H2 ✉ Place du Monastère, avenue des Arènes ⏰ Daylight hours 🚌 15, 17, 20, 22
♿ Very good ✋ Free

### MONASTÈRE FRANCISCAIN DE CIMIEZ

At the northern end of the Parc des Arènes, the church of the Franciscan monastery dates from the 15th century. Its highlights include three paintings by the Nice-born Gothic painter Louis Bréa, the marble Séraphic cross of 1477, and a magnificent carved-wood altarpiece adorned with gold leaf. The vaulted ceiling is covered with frescoes depicting the life of St. Francis. The Franciscan Museum in the adjoining monastery building has displays on the life of the religious brothers in Nice from the 13th to 18th centuries. Be sure to walk through the Old Monastery Garden, with its bright flower beds, rose gardens, pergolas and mature trees. There are shady benches from which to enjoy the superb views across to the Baie des Anges.

✚ J2 ✉ Place du Monastère ☎ 04 93 81 00 04 ⏰ Church: daily 8–6.30. Museum: May to mid-Oct Mon–Sat 10–noon, 3–6; mid-Oct to end Apr Mon–Sat 10–noon, 3–5.30 🚌 15, 17, 20, 22 ♿ Few ✋ Free

*An exhibit in the Franciscan Museum*
*A bust of jazz musician Lionel Hampton, in the Jardin des Arènes de Cimiez*

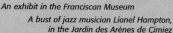

# Farther Afield

Nice is the gateway to the Côte d'Azur. Discover the glamour of Cannes, the perfumeries of Grasse, medieval hilltop villages and exotic gardens.

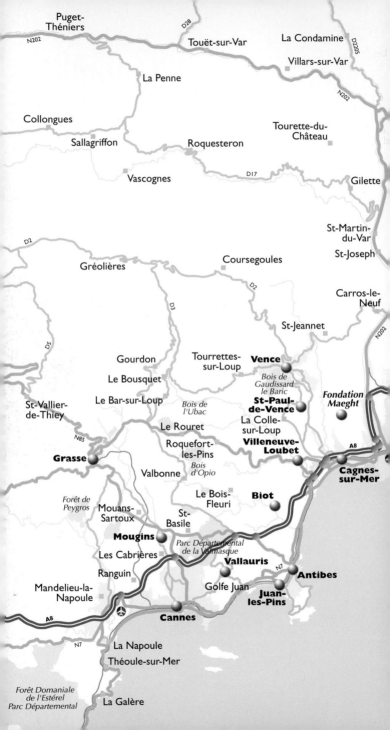

Lantosque

D70

Les Condamines

Peïra-Cava

Moulinet

Parc National
du Mercantour

Le Cros-
d'Utelle

Duranus

D21

Lucéram

D2566

Sospel

D204

Levens
La Madone

Berre-les-
Alpes

Touët-de-
l'Escarène

Castillon

D2566a

Plan
d'Arriou

Peille

Tourrette-
Levens

Colomars

Cantaron
Drap

Laghet

A8

Roquebrune-
Cap-Martin

Menton

La Turbie

Èze

Monte-Carlo

St-Antoine-
Ginestière

Eze-Bord
de Mer

Monaco-Ville
Monaco

Cap-d'Ail

NICE

N98

Beaulieu-sur-Mer
Villefranche-sur-Mer
Villa Ephrussi
de Rothschild

St-Jean-
Cap-Ferrat

I

0        5 km

0        3 miles

# Antibes

---

### HIGHLIGHTS

● The ramparts
● Musée Picasso

### TIP

● 'The Painters of the Côte d'Azur' is a self-guided route around the Riviera where panels have been placed to show the viewpoints that inspired famous paintings. In Antibes you'll find five panels along the coast beyond Bastion St-André. Ask at the tourist office for a brochure.

**Antibes has an attractive old town filled with lively squares, but the best way to get a feel for its former glory is to walk along the massive 17th-century ramparts that stretch along the seafront.**

**Nice's rival** Antibes was founded as a Greek trading post in the 5th century BC and named Antipolis ('Opposite the City'), as it faced Nice. It became a key player in medieval times as the French counterpoint to the Savoy kingdom at Nice. Fort Carré, which stands on the Saint-Roch peninsula separating Antibes from the Baie des Anges, was built in the 16th century and was strengthened by Vauban, Louis XIV's military architect, around 1680. The town's ramparts were added at this time. Below the fort is Port Vauban, the largest yacht marina in Europe. You can walk along the

*Clockwise from left: sunbathing on the beach; the tower of the Château Grimaldi; the shingle beach of Port de l'Olivette, one of many coves on Cap d'Antibes; a market stall on the Cours Masséna; a pasta restaurant; the gilded wooden statue of Notre-Dame-de-Bon-Port (Our Lady of Safe Homecoming), in the Sanctuaire de la Garoupe*

ramparts from the old port to the Bastion St-André, which houses the archaeology museum.

**The old town** The highlight of the old town, Vieil Antibes, is Château Grimaldi, rebuilt in the 16th century and now home to the Musée Picasso. Picasso rented a room here in 1946, and the ceramics and paintings he produced form the basis of the museum. There are also works by Nicholas de Staël, Germaine Richier and other artists. Next door is the baroque cathedral. Behind it is the wonderful covered Provençal market on Cours Masséna. Lined with shops and shuttered stone houses, the old town streets lead to pleasant squares. Plage de la Gravette is a small beach near the old port, with larger beaches stretching south from the ramparts. Beyond is the peninsula of Cap d'Antibes, with its posh villas.

**THE BASICS**

www.antibesjuanlespins.com

✚ Off map to west along seafront

🛈 11 place de Gaulle, tel 04 92 90 53 00; Jul, Aug Mon–Sun 9–7; Sep–end Jun Mon–Fri 9–12.30, 1.30–6, Sat 9–noon, 2–6

🍴 Cafés, bars, restaurants

🚌 200

🚆 Antibes

❓ The Musée Picasso is due to reopen some time in 2008, after renovation

# Cannes

## HIGHLIGHTS

- La Croisette
- Le Suquet
- Musée de la Castre
- View from Saracen tower
- Ste-Marguerite

## TIPS

- Spot the murals inspired by movies, on buildings throughout town.
- Shady paths wind through the pine and eucalyptus forests of Ste-Marguerite. There are beaches, too, so pack a picnic and spend a few hours at this retreat.

**Cannes is best known for its Film Festival, when celebrities walk the red carpet into the Palais des Festivals; but the most stellar view is the panorama from the top of the castle tower.**

**Movie magic** For most of the year the Palais des Festivals is simply a convention centre. But for 11 days each May, it is the most glamorous place on earth as film stars descend for the *Festival de Cannes*, Europe's most prestigious cinema event. The Palais sits alongside the Vieux Port, a sprawling marina filled with luxury yachts. To the east is La Croisette, the palm-lined promenade that stretches along Cannes' sandy beaches, a popular spot for strolling and celebrity-spotting. Across the road are luxury shops and grand hotels, such as the Carlton and

*Clockwise from top left: boats moored in the harbour; Cannes' old town is crowned by a medieval castle; flags from luxury yachts flutter in the breeze; Meryl Streep's hand-print in the 'allée des Stars', on La Croisette; flowers on sale in the Marché Forville; the Hôtel Martinez*

Majestic. The shopping streets behind La Croisette lead west to the Marché Forville, a covered market. From here narrow streets wind uphill into Le Suquet, Cannes' old quarter, where there are lively bars and restaurants.

**Castles and islands** Crowning the hill of the old town, the medieval castle now houses the Musée de la Castre. It has small but impressive collections of pre-Colombian ceramics, Mediterranean antiquities, South Pacific masks and musical instruments from around the world. Climb the 11th-century Saracen tower (built to watch for invaders) for spectacular views. From the port, take a short boat ride to the Îles de Lérins, where you can explore a fortress and nature trails on Ste-Marguerite or the monastery on St-Honorat.

## THE BASICS

www.cannes.fr

🔀 Off map to west along seafront

🛈 Palais des Festivals, La Croisette, tel 04 92 99 84 22; Jul, Aug daily 9–8; Sep–end Jun daily 9–7

🍽 Cafés, bars and restaurants

🚌 200

🚉 Cannes

🚢 Excursion boats to Les Îles de Lérins run all year (expensive)

❓ Musée de la Castre is open Tue–Sun (also Mon Jul, Aug)

# Cagnes-sur-Mer

*The Grimaldi Castle dominates the medieval streets of Haut-de-Cagnes*

## THE BASICS

www.cagnes-tourisme.com
➕ Off map to west along seafront
ℹ️ 6 boulevard Maréchal Juin, tel 04 93 20 61 64; Jul, Aug Mon–Sat 9–7, Sun 9–noon, 3–7; Jun, Sep Mon–Sat 9–noon, 2–7; Oct–end May Mon–Sat 9–noon, 2–6
🍴 Cafés, bars and restaurants
🚌 200, 400,
🚉 Cagnes-sur-Mer, Cros-de-Cagnes
❓ Museums open Wed–Mon

## HIGHLIGHTS

● Musée Renoir
● Haut-de-Cagnes
● View from the Grimaldi Castle tower
● 16th-century frescoes in the chapel of Notre-Dame de la Protection (open only on guided tours from the tourist office)

**Don't be put off by the busy town centre. From its shiny new seafront promenade to its hilltop medieval village, to Renoir's peaceful olive garden, Cagnes-sur-Mer shows several faces of the Riviera.**

**Three in one** There are three parts to this resort. On the seafront is Cros-de-Cagnes, set around the old fishermen's village. To either side a broad promenade runs for 3km (2 miles) along the beach. At its west end it fronts the Hippodrome, the largest racecourse on the Côte d'Azur. Slightly inland is the commercial heart of Cagnes-sur-Mer. From here you can take a free shuttle bus to Haut-de-Cagnes, the medieval village on the hilltop.

**Renoir's garden** A short walk or bus ride from downtown brings you to the Musée Renoir. It is in the artist's last home, Les Collettes, surrounded by an ancient olive grove. A master Impressionist, Pierre-Auguste Renoir bought the farm in 1907 and built the villa where, crippled with rheumatoid arthritis, he continued to paint until his death in 1919. His studio remains as he left it, and you can see many original paintings.

**Medieval treasure** The peaceful medieval streets of Haut-de-Cagnes are a world away from the busy resort below. At the highest point the Grimaldi Castle, dating from 1300, has beautiful loggias and a monumental staircase. Its ornate rooms house modern art exhibitions, the olive tree museum and 40 portraits of Suzy Solidor, cabaret singer and muse to many artists.

*Èze offers wonderful views of the coast (left) and pretty cobbled streets (right)*

# Èze

**With possibly the most stunning viewpoint on the Riviera, you're unlikely to enjoy Èze in solitude. But catch a quiet moment and this perched village casts its medieval magic once again.**

**Eagle's nest** Clinging to the summit of a rocky outcrop 429m (1,400ft) above the sea, Èze is one of the most dramatic perched villages in Provence. Settlements have been here since the Bronze Age, but it acquired its maze of winding passages and stairways in medieval times, when it was fortified under various rulers. Today the stone houses are almost entirely given over to tourism, with galleries and souvenir shops cheek by jowl along many of the picturesque lanes. The Chapel of the White Penitents is the oldest building in the village, dating from 1306. The Château de la Chèvre d'Or is now a luxury hotel with a gastronomic restaurant (▷ 106). The plain façade of the Church of Notre-Dame de l'Assomption, built 1764–1772, conceals splendid baroque decoration inside.

**Exotic Gardens** At the very top of the village, the Jardin Exotique gives the most dramatic views over the coastline from St-Jean-Cap-Ferrat to Monaco. It is on the site of a Moorish fortress, destroyed by Louis XIV's soldiers in 1706. It winding paths are lined with cacti, agave, rare shrubs and succulent plants, and sculptures of Earth Goddesses by Jean-Philippe Richard. If you're up for a strenuous walk, follow the Chemin de Nietzsche, a steep, narrow path between Èze and its seaside counterpart, Èze-sur-Mer, used by the German philosopher in 1883.

## THE BASICS

www.eze-riviera.com
🔠 Off map to east along seafront
🚩 Place du Général de Gaulle, tel 04 93 41 26 00; Apr–end Oct daily 9–7; Nov–end Mar Mon–Sat 9–6
🍴 Cafés, bars and restaurants
🚌 82
❓ Jardin Exotique open daily; admission moderate

## HIGHLIGHTS

● Jardin Exotique
● Stunning coastal views

## TIP

● The Chemin de Nietzsche is very steep and rough, and you'll need good walking shoes and plenty of water with you.

# Fondation Maeght

*The Cour Alberto Giacometti of the Fondation Maeght (left); indoor gallery space (right)*

## THE BASICS

www.fondation-maeght.com

- 🔄 Off map to west
- ✉ St-Paul-de-Vence
- ☎ 04 93 32 81 63
- 🕐 Jul–end Sep daily 10–7; Oct–end Jun daily 10–12.30, 2.30–6
- 🍽 Café
- 🚌 400
- ♿ Good
- 👊 Expensive

## HIGHLIGHTS

- Sculpture garden
- Miró's Egg
- Giacometti terrace

**At this outstanding museum, leading artists of the 20th century have created a whimsical world, with monumental sculptures set outdoors among the pines.**

**Artist friends** The Fondation Marguerite et Aimé Maeght, in St-Paul-de-Vence, is one of the leading private art galleries of the world. Aimé Maeght was an art dealer, printer, editor and film producer who became friends with all the leading artists working in the south of France after World War II, including Bonnard, Miró, Braque and Chagall. They collaborated on the creation of this unique gallery, which was built to house the Maeghts' extensive private collection. Catalan architect José Luis Sert designed the airy building, which blends into the surrounding landscape and opens onto terraces and courtyards that are integral parts of the exhibition space.

**Garden gallery** The highlights are spread around the grounds, on a shady hillside beneath towering pines. Bright Calder mobiles and fanciful figures by Miró, some monumental in size, are spread throughout the lawns and terraces. Elongated statues people the Giacometti courtyard. Water spouts through Picasso's whimsical fountain faces and Pol Bury's tubular fountain. Mosaics by Chagall and stained glass by Braque adorn the library and chapel. Inside the building, paintings, sculptures, drawings and graphic art from the permanent collection are shown on a rotating basis, though much space is devoted to the annual summer exhibition.

*Stock up on some perfume (left) or just enjoy a wander in the old town (right)*

**Grasse is famous as the perfume capital of the world, but wander through the narrow backstreets and you'll discover a fascinating medieval town.**

**Scents of adventure** Grasse's perfume industry started in 1580, when the town's tanners developed a technique for making perfumed leather gloves. Surrounded by abundant flower fields, the business thrived and the city has been the leading hub of perfume-making ever since. The Musée International de la Parfumerie presents an innovative look at all aspects of perfume making. Three perfumeries—Fragonard, Galimard and Molinard—offer free guided tours of their factories, which explain the process of perfume creation. Only Fragonard has a location in the middle of town, with an adjoining museum.

**Follow your nose** From the arcades of the place aux Aires, where tanners once spread out their hides, follow the winding streets of the old town. Look out for plaques identifying notable medieval buildings, and for panels of the 'Painters of the Côte d'Azur' route (▷ 82). The cathedral has three paintings by Rubens and the only religious painting by Jean-Honoré Fragonard. Born in Grasse, he found fame painting romantic scenes for Louis XV's court. The Fragonard perfumerie was named in his honour by founders the Fuchs family. The Villa-Musée Fragonard contains copies of his large-scale series *The Progress of Love in the Heart of a Young Lady*. The Museum of Art and History of Provence is also worth a visit.

---

## THE BASICS

www.grasse.fr

➕ Off map to west

🏠 Place du Cours Honoré Cresp and place de la Foux, tel 04 93 36 03 56/ 04 93 36 21 68;
Jul–end Sep Mon–Sat 9–7, Sun 9–1, 2–6; Oct–end Jun Mon–Sat 9–12.30, 2–6

🍴 Cafés, bars and restaurants

🚍 500

🚉 Grasse

❓ Perfumeries open daily; admission free. Museums closed Tue Oct–end May; admission inexpensive–moderate

---

## HIGHLIGHTS

● Musée International de la Parfumerie
● Fragonard Museum and tour
● The medieval town

# Monaco-Ville

**Monaco-Ville, the oldest part of the
tiny principality of Monaco, is the most
extraordinary of the French Riviera's
'perched villages'.**

**The Rock** The independent state of Monaco,
which covers just 195ha (485 acres), has been
ruled by the Grimaldi family since the 14th century.
Famous as a gambling hub, tax haven and site of
the Grand Prix, it has long attracted the wealthy
and the glamorous. But it captured the imagination
of the world in 1956 with the fairytale marriage of
its late monarch, Prince Rainier III, to Hollywood
star Grace Kelly. Monaco-Ville, the old fortified
town, sits high above the sea on the peninsula
known as The Rock. At its heart is the palace and
the enormous palace square, where the changing
of the guard takes place daily at 11.55 sharp. You

Monaco-Ville is the principality's old fortified town, built around the Palais Princier, home to the monarch

can see the gorgeous state apartments of the Palais Princier on a self-guided tour.

**Sea to sky** The narrow streets of the surrounding old town lead to the cathedral, built of white stone from La Turbie. Behind the altar are the tombs of Princess Grace, who died tragically in a car accident on the Corniche in 1982, and Prince Rainier. Stroll through the lovely St-Martins Gardens, opposite, which run along the side of the Rock to the Musée Océanographique and its fabulous Aquarium, with its shark lagoon and fascinating marine species.

**Farther out** Take bus No. 2 to the Jardin Exotique, outside the old town at the top of Monaco, where an amazing range of exotic cacti and succulents reach for the sky along winding paths.

**THE BASICS**

www.visitmonaco.com
🖿 Off map to east along seafront
🚹 2 boulevard des Moulins, Monte-Carlo, tel 04 92 16 61 16; Mon–Sat 9–7, Sun 10–noon
🍴 Cafés, bars and restaurants
🚌 100
🚉 Monaco-Monte-Carlo
❓ Palace, Aquarium and Exotic Gardens open daily; admission moderate–expensive

# Monte-Carlo

*Monte-Carlo's famous casino (left); high-rise buildings behind the harbour (right)*

## THE BASICS

www.visitmonaco.com

🚩 Off map to east along seafront

ℹ️ 2 boulevard des Moulins, Monte-Carlo, tel 04 92 16 61 16; Mon–Sat 9–7, Sun 10–noon

🍴 Cafés, bars and restaurants

🚌 100

🚉 Monaco–Monte-Carlo

❓ Casino is open Mon–Fri 2pm–6am, Sat, Sun noon–6am; admission expensive. No one under 18 is admitted and ID is required. To arrange a tour, contact the casino 1–2 weeks in advance. Smart dress advised; jacket and tie required for entry to private rooms

## HIGHLIGHTS

● The Casino
● A drink at the Café de Paris
● Window shopping

**The best way to soak up the glamour of Monte-Carlo is to have a drink at the outdoor terrace of the Café de Paris. Here you can watch the comings and goings around the place du Casino.**

**The Legend** Monte-Carlo is Monaco's wealthiest and most glamorous district. It was created in 1866 and named after Prince Charles III, who had founded the Casino three years earlier to establish an economic base for the principality. The gamble paid off. The Casino was an immediate success, and in 1878 it was remodelled and enlarged by Charles Garnier. Ever more elaborate rooms were added and embellished by other architects over the years. The Roaring Twenties brought aristocrats and celebrities to Monte-Carlo, and by 1950 the world's high rollers preferred the Casino's gaming tables to any other. It is still known as The Legend. It's worth the entry fee just to see the Casino's opulent interior, adorned with crystal chandeliers, onyx columns, marble floors, friezes and ceiling frescoes. Highlights include Garnier's lavish European Room, the American Room (1903) and Les Salles Touzet (1889).

**Luxury living** Expensive jewellers and designer boutiques line Monte-Carlo's main street, boulevard des Moulins. The Larvotto area has man-made beaches and swimming facilities. For sports clubs, beach clubs and nightclubs, head to Avenue Princess-Grace. If you're not a motor racing fan, avoid the week of the Grand Prix, when roads are closed and crowds are at their peak.

*Nine themed gardens
surround the ornate,
pink Villa Ephrussi*

**TOP 25**

# Villa Ephrussi de Rothschild

**Behind this beautiful pink villa, magnificent themed gardens stretch along the top of St-Jean-Cap-Ferrat. Best of all are the magical musical fountains. They may make you smile, embrace or even dance.**

**Passionate collector** Baroness Béatrice Ephrussi de Rothschild bought these 7ha (17 acres) atop the peninsula in 1905 and built this sumptuous pink palace modelled on the Renaissance villas of Italy. She personally designed the ornate villa, using a recurring rose theme and the colour pink. A passionate traveller, she named it the *Île de France*, after a luxury liner on which she had sailed. The wealthy heiress was an avid art collector and filled the villa with her treasures. The ground floor rooms surround a covered patio with pink marble colonnades, galleries and Moorish arches. They contain priceless antique furniture, including Marie-Antoinette's whist table, and a fine porcelain collection. The collections on the upper floor can be seen only on a guided tour.

**Glorious gardens** Nine themed gardens evoke exotic destinations. The main French garden is designed to resemble a ship's deck, with the Temple of Love at the prow. At the start of the long pond are magnificent musical fountains that perform their mesmerizing dance every 10 minutes. The gardens wind along the narrow peninsula, with splendid sea views, to the rose garden at the end. In between are Provençal, Japanese, Florentine, Spanish and Stone gardens, with patios, ponds, statues and exotic plants.

## THE BASICS

www.culturespaces.com
✛ Off map to east along seafront
✉ St-Jean-Cap-Ferrat
☎ 04 93 01 33 09
🕐 Jul, Aug daily 10–7; mid-Feb to end Jun, Sep to mid-Nov daily 10–6; mid-Nov to mid-Feb Mon–Fri 2–6, Sat, Sun and school hols 10–6
🍴 Restaurant
🚌 81
🚊 Beaulieu-sur-Mer
♿ Good
💰 Expensive
❓ Additional fee (inexpensive) for guided tours of the collections; book early at reception as numbers are limited.
A combined ticket for the Villa Kérylos (▷ 95) and Villa Ephrussi is available

## HIGHLIGHTS

● The covered patio in the villa
● The musical fountains
● The Stone garden
● The French garden

# Villefranche-sur-Mer

*Picturesque Villefranche-sur-Mer is the deep-water port for Nice*

## THE BASICS

www.villefranche-sur-mer.com

🔁 Off map to east along seafront

ℹ️ Jardin François-Binon, tel 04 93 01 73 68; Jul, Aug daily 9–7; Jun, Sep Mon–Sat 9–noon, 2–6.30; Oct–end May Mon–Sat 9–noon, 2–6

🍴 Cafés, bars and restaurants

🚌 100

🚉 Villefranche-sur-Mer

❓ Chapelle St-Pierre is open Tue–Sun 10–noon, 3–7; admission inexpensive. The castle museums are closed lunchtimes and Sun Sep–end Jun; admission free

## HIGHLIGHTS

● Waterfront façades
● Chapelle St-Pierre
● Rue Obscure
● Musée Volti in the castle ramparts

**With its brightly painted façades of orange, yellow and red forming a semi-circle around the harbour, Villefranche is one of the prettiest towns on the Côte d'Azur.**

**Picturesque port** Fishing craft tie up and pile their nets along the narrow, cobblestoned quay-side, selling their fresh catch straight off the boat. Villefranche serves as the deep-water port for Nice and cruise ships anchor farther out in the bay, disgorging hundreds of passengers onto tour buses waiting below the castle. The artist Jean Cocteau was a regular visitor here and decorated Chapelle St-Pierre, the tiny medieval fishermen's chapel beside the harbour. Every inch of the interior is covered with his expressive frescoes, while giant candlestick pillars topped by watchful eyes guard the door.

**Charming town** Steep steps lead up from the waterfront into the old town, on the slope above. Partway along rue de l'Eglise is the start of the long, atmospheric vaulted medieval passageway called rue Obscure, where residents sheltered during attacks from the 14th century onwards. It makes an eerie contrast to the colourful façades along the waterfront. At the top of town is the Église St-Michel. Farther west is the 16th-century castle. You can walk around its massive ramparts, and cross the drawbridge to enter its wooden gates. Inside is the town hall and several small art museums, the best of which houses sensual sculptures by the local artist Antoniucci Volti.

## BEAULIEU-SUR-MER

www.ot-beaulieu-sur-mer.fr

This pretty resort on the east side of St-Jean-Cap-Ferrat (▷ 97) has a genteel charm, with its elegant Rotonde, casino and palm-lined gardens facing the sea. Its star attraction is the Villa Kérylos, a reconstruction of a wealthy house from the Greek island of Delos around the 2nd century BC. It was built in 1902–08 by archaeologist Theodore Reinach. The villa occupies a beautiful spot on the eastern end of the Bay of Fourmis, which has a sandy beach backed by a promenade. You can follow the promenade to the pink seaside villa once owned by David Niven. From there you can walk uphill to Villa Ephrussi (▷ 93).

🔛 Off map to east along seafront 🚹 Place Georges Clémenceau, tel 04 93 01 02 21; open daily in summer 🍴 Cafes, bars, restaurants 🚊 Beaulieu-sur-Mer

**Villa Kérylos** ✉ Impasse Gustave Eiffel ☎ 04 93 01 01 44 🕐 Jul, Aug daily 10–7; mid-Feb to end Jun, Sep to mid-Nov daily 10–6; mid-Nov to mid-Feb Mon–Fri 2–6, Sat, Sun and school hols 10–6

## BIOT

www.biot.fr

This medieval hilltop town was resettled by Italians after the plague wiped out most of its original inhabitants, thus giving it its unusual pronunciation (Bee-ot). Another legacy is the lovely loggias that surround the place des Arcades. Picturesque cobbled streets fan out from here, lined with boutiques, galleries, bars and cafés. Biot is a thriving arts and crafts hub, known for its potteries and glassworks. Watch glass-blowers making the town's distinctive 'bubble glass', *verre bullé*, at the Verrerie de Biot. Outside the old town, the Musée Fernand Léger houses several hundred of Léger's paintings, ceramics, murals and stained glass. Next door is the tranquil Bonsai Arboretum.

🔛 Off map to west 🚹 46 rue St-Sébastien, tel 04 93 65 78 00; Jul, Aug Mon–Fri 10–7, Sat, Sun 2.30–7; Sep–end Jun Mon–Fri 9–noon, 2–6, Sat, Sun 2–6 🍴 Cafés, bars, restaurants 🚊 Antibes, then bus 10 to village ❓ Musée Léger closed for renovation at time of writing

*Pottery is a good buy in Biot*

*The harbour at Beaulieu-sur-Mer*

## JUAN-LES-PINS

www.antibesjuanlespins.com

In the 1920s Juan-les-Pins was the first resort to stay open in summer, at a time when holidaying in the summer was something of a novelty. With Picasso, Coco Chanel and F. Scott Fitzgerald among its visitors, Juan-les-Pins and nearby Antibes made the Côte d'Azur a chic, year-round playground. The fine sandy beach is backed by a beautiful grove of mature pines, known as La Pinède, which hosts the renowned summer jazz festival. The resort's clubs and bars offer some of the region's best nightlife.

➕ Off map to west along seafront 🛈 51 boulevard Guillaumont, tel 04 92 90 53 05; Jul, Aug daily 9–7; Sep–end Jun Mon–Fri 9–noon, 2–6, Sat 9–noon 🍴 Cafés, bars, restaurants 🚉 Juan-les-Pins

## MENTON

www.menton.fr

A stone's throw from the Italian border, Menton is known for its balmy climate, the warmest on the Riviera, and its lemons, which are celebrated with fabulous floats and citrus displays during the annual *Fête du Citron*, a two-week Lemon Festival held in February. The mountains encircling the town help create a subtropical microclimate, and there are many lush gardens that can be visited. The steep streets of the old town, with tall, sun-bleached houses and baroque churches, rise up from the pretty harbour, which is backed by a palm-lined promenade. A popular attraction is the Salle des Mariages (Wedding Hall) in the town hall, decorated with wonderful murals by Jean Cocteau. The Musée Jean Cocteau displays a variety of his works in a small 17th-century bastion by the waterfront. Palais Carnolès, once the summer home of the princes of Monaco, now houses the Musée des Beaux-Arts.

➕ Off map to east along seafront 🛈 Palais de l'Europe, 8 avenue Boyer, tel 04 92 41 76 76; mid-Jun to mid-Sep daily 9–7; mid-Sep to mid-Jun Mon–Sat 8.30–12.30, 2–6, Sun 9–12.30 🍴 Cafés, bars, restaurants 🚉 Menton ❓ Salle des Mariages open Mon–Fri 8.30–12.30, 2–5 (inexpensive)

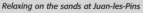

*Relaxing on the sands at Juan-les-Pins*

*Menton's vibrant* **Fête du Citron**

## MOUGINS

www.mougins-coteazur.org

Picasso lived in this hilltop village for the last 12 years of his life. Pictures of him are displayed in the Musée de la Photographie. Today the village is home to wealthy residents as well as artists, and is full of galleries and fine restaurants. The old laundry, Le Lavoir, is an exhibition space for local art.

🔢 Off map to the west 🚌 15 avenue Jean Charles Mallet, 04 93 75 87 67; Jul, Aug daily 9–8.30; Sep–end Jun Mon–Sat 9–5.30 🍴 Cafés, bars, restaurants 🚊 Cannes, then bus 600

## ROQUEBRUNE-CAP-MARTIN

www.roquebrune-cap-martin.com

A labyrinth of stairways, narrow lanes and vaulted passageways runs through the old fortified village of Roquebrune, which lies between Menton and Monaco. At the top you can visit the 10th-century Château de Roquebrune. The village is perched above beautiful Cap Martin, with its lush carpet of olive, pine and mimosa trees. Royalty and celebrities built secluded villas here in the 20th century, including the architect Le Corbusier. A coastal path around the promontory is named after him.

🔢 Off map to east along seafront 🚌 218 avenue Aristide Briand, tel 04 93 35 62 87; Jul, Aug Mon–Sat 9–1, 3–7, Sun 10–1, 3–7; Sep–end Jun Mon–Sat 9–12.30, 2–6 🍴 Cafés, bars, restaurants 🚊 Roquebrune-Cap-Martin

## ST-JEAN-CAP-FERRAT

www.saintjeancapferrat.fr

The beautiful promontory between Villefranche-sur-Mer and Beaulieu-sur-Mer is known as the Peninsula of Billionaires. Though wealth rules in the handsome villas of Cap Ferrat and the former fishing port of St-Jean, the glorious coastal path and its beaches are free to all. Villa Ephrussi de Rothschild (▷ 93) is a top attraction.

🔢 Off map to east along seafront 🚌 59 avenue Denis Semeria, tel 04 93 76 08 90; Jul, Aug daily 8.30–6.30; Sep–end Jun Mon–Fri 8.30–6, Sat 9–5 🍴 Cafés, bars, restaurants 🚊 Beaulieu-sur-Mer, then a 15-minute walk

*White shutters on Le Manoir de l'Etang restaurant and hotel, in Mougins*

*The harbour at St-Jean*

## ST-PAUL-DE-VENCE

www.saint-pauldevence.com

This stunning medieval perched village, entirely surrounded by its 16th-century walls, is one of the most visited spots on the Côte d'Azur. It was a magnet for artists, including Braque, Miró and Picasso, who left paintings in the famous Colombe d'Or hotel and restaurant (▷ 106). Marc Chagall lived here for 20 years and is buried in the cemetery. Today the pretty, cobbled streets are lined with art galleries. Walk around the ramparts for stunning views. You can visit the church, parts of which date from the 13th century, the history museum in the castle keep and the White Penitents' Chapel, newly renovated with a mosaic and stained glass designed by the artist Folon. A 10-minute walk outside the walls brings you to Fondation Maeght (▷ 88).

➕ Off map to west  📋 2 rue Grande, tel 04 93 32 86 95; Jun–end Sep Mon–Fri 10–7, Sat, Sun 10–1, 2–7; Oct–end May daily 10–noon, 1–6  🍴 Cafés, bars, restaurants  🚌 400

## LA TURBIE

Towering over this small village on the Grande Corniche is the Trophée des Alpes, erected to glorify the Roman emperor Augustus who conquered the region in the 1st century BC. The monument, with its Doric columns, is built of the same white local stone used for Monaco's cathedral. The monument's statue of Augustus, shown in a scale model in the museum, disappeared long ago.

➕ Off map to east  🍴 Cafés, bars, restaurants  🚌 116

**Trophée des Alpes**  ✉ Avenue Albert I  ☎ 04 93 41 20 84  🕐 Mid-May to mid-Sep 9.30–1, 2.30–6.30; mid-Sep to mid-May 10–1.30, 2.30–5  🚌 116  ✋ Moderate

## VALLAURIS

www.vallauris-golfe-juan.com

Picasso spent two years here producing his distinctive ceramics. In 1949 he decorated the medieval chapel in the castle courtyard with murals of War and Peace. It's now the Musée National Picasso. A few of Picasso's ceramics are displayed in the Musée

*The Trophée des Alpes towers above La Turbie's old town*
*A narrow street in St-Paul-de-Vence*

Magnelli-Musée de la Céramique next door. Avenue Georges-Clemenceau, lined with pottery shops, runs downhill to the Galerie Madoura (▷ 102), which produces limited editions of Picasso's designs.

⊞ Off map to west 🛈 Square du 8 mai 1945, tel 04 93 63 82 58; Jul, Aug daily 9–7; Sep–end Jun Mon–Sat 9–noon, 2–6 🍴 Cafés, bars, restaurants 🚌 Golfe Juan, then bus 20 to place de la Libération

## VENCE

www.vence.fr

Medieval walls encircle much of the old town centre of Vence, a 10-minute bus ride from St-Paul-de-Vence. A mosaic by Chagall hangs in the cathedral. D.H. Lawrence died here in 1930, and there is a memorial plaque in the cemetery. Vence's most famous resident was Henri Matisse, who moved here during World War II. Between 1947 and 1951 he decorated the Chapelle du Rosaire for the Dominican sisters, as a thank you to one of the nuns who had nursed him during an illness. The chapel, a 20-minute walk from the heart of town, is beautiful and peaceful, illuminated by its white walls and the light streaming through the stained-glass windows. Matisse called the chapel 'my masterpiece—what I have made most beautiful during my whole life'.

⊞ Off map to west 🛈 8 place du Grand Jardin, tel 04 93 58 06 38; Jul, Aug Mon–Sat 9–7, Sun 9–1; Sep–end Jun Mon–Sat 9–6 🍴 Cafés, restaurants 🚌 400, 94 ❓ Chapelle du Rosaire open Mon, Wed, Sat 2–5.30, Tue, Thu 10–11.30, 2–5.30

## VILLENEUVE-LOUBET

www.ot-villeneuveloubet.org

This is the birthplace of master chef Auguste Escoffier (1846–1935). The Musée Escoffier de l'Art Culinaire has menus, photos and culinary displays showcasing his dishes. Don't confuse this attractive inland village with the coastal Villeneuve-Loubet Plage.

⊞ Off map to west 🛈 Rue de l'Hôtel de Ville, tel 04 93 20 16 49; Jul, Aug Mon–Sat 9.30–12.30, 3–7; Sep–end Jun Mon–Fri 9–noon, 3–6, Sat 9.30–12.30 🍴 Cafés, bars, restaurants 🚌 500

*Enjoying a drink in Vence's old town*

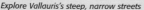

*Explore Vallauris's steep, narrow streets*

# Old Antibes

Take in the highlights of old Antibes, from its picturesque medieval streets to the massive ramparts running along the sea.

**DISTANCE:** 1.6km (1 mile)  **ALLOW:** 1.5 hours

**START**

**TOURIST OFFICE, PLACE GÉNÉRAL DE GAULLE**

**END**

**BASTION ST-ANDRÉ**

**1** Start at the tourist information office and walk straight ahead past the playful fountains in place Général de Gaulle.

**8** Return to the ramparts and follow the promenade to its end at Bastion St-André. Beyond is the pretty Square Albert I, with fine views back towards the ramparts, and a string of sandy beaches.

**2** Turn left at the end, cross the intersection beside the bus station, and continue down rue de la République.

**7** After Château Grimaldi, detour right at place du Barri, which leads to the market in Cours Masséna.

**3** At the end of the street, beside place Nationale, turn left into rue Thuret, passing the pretty little fountain square.

**6** Return through Porte Marine and veer left at place Malespine, up Rampe des Saleurs to Promenade Amiral de Grasse, which runs along the ramparts.

**4** At the end of rue Thuret, turn right into boulevard d'Aguillon. Just past another fountain, turn left and walk through Porte Marine, the ancient gate in the ramparts, to the Vieux Port.

**5** You can extend the walk by strolling along the quays of the old port, or around the enormous Port Vauban.

**FARTHER AFIELD**  **WALK**

# Shopping

## Antibes

### BALADE EN PROVENCE
Beneath the arcades in the Marché Provençal, this shop sells a great range of regional food and drink, such as wines, olives, oils and something rather unusual—a selection of absinthes. Have a look at the absinthe bar in the basement.
🔲 Off map to west ✉ 25 Cours Masséna, Antibes ☎ 04 93 34 93 00 🚊 Antibes

### LE BAZAR DE L'HÔTEL DE VILLE
This friendly shop in the Marché Provençal is piled high with baskets of all shapes, sizes and styles. You can't miss it as they are hung prettily along the façade and around the doorway.
🔲 Off map to west ✉ 27 Cours Masséna, Antibes ☎ 04 93 34 32 01 🚊 Antibes

### DMC
This shop has a great range of stylish shoes and sandals, including the very comfortable Mephisto brand.
🔲 Off map to west ✉ 38 rue de la République, Antibes ☎ 04 97 21 69 31 🚊 Antibes

### L'EMPEREUR
www.emperor.fr
The emperor here is an ex-rugby player from Gascony, Jérôme Verrier, who shares his love of foie gras and confits de canard by offering this selection of the finest from the southwest of France, along with Armagnac and Bordeaux wines.
🔲 Off map to west ✉ 7 Cours Masséna, Antibes ☎ 04 93 34 04 86 🚊 Antibes

### HEIDI'S ENGLISH BOOKSHOP
Heidi's is a lifeline for English-speaking book-worms on the Côte d'Azur, with the latest fiction, nonfiction, art books, cookery books, maps and travel guides, as well as used books. It's a great place to pick up a holiday read.
🔲 Off map to west ✉ 24 rue Aubernon, Antibes ☎ 04 93 34 74 11 🚊 Antibes

---

### FRUIT AND FLOWERS
Fruit, flowers and a famous family link two of the Côte d'Azur's top products: confectionery and perfume. In 1949 Georges Fuchs, son of Fragonard founder Eugène Fuchs, converted a perfumery at Le Pont du Loup, between Grasse and Vence, into the Confiserie des Gorges du Loup and began producing candied fruits, jams and crystallised flowers. With the purchase of a Nice chocolate factory in 1972, the business became Confiserie Florian. You can visit both branches (www.confiserieflorian.com).

---

## Biot

### GALERIE FARINELLI
www.farinelli.fr
Master glassmaker Raphaël Farinelli grew up in Biot and learned his craft here. His distinctive tableware is sold in this shop in the middle of town and at his workshop on 465 route de la Mer.
🔲 Off map to west ✉ 24 rue Sébastien Saint, Biot ☎ 04 93 65 01 89 🚊 Antibes, then bus 10 to village

### VERRERIE DE BIOT
www.verreriebiot.com
The unique bubble glass-ware known as verre bullé was invented at this studio. After watching it being made, you can buy pieces in the shop or order them online.
🔲 Off map to west ✉ Chemin des Combes, Biot ☎ 04 93 65 33 00 🚊 Antibes, then bus 10 to village

## Cannes

### EDEN GRAY
Fine linen and luxurious lin-gerie, with such brands as La Perla and Eres, make for a sensual splurge at this lovely shop.
🔲 Off map to west ✉ 17 La Croisette, Cannes ☎ 04 93 99 58 11 🚊 Cannes

### FROMAGERIE CENERI
You'll find cheeses from all over France in this family-run shop. They are aged in the shop's own cellar.
🔲 Off map to west ✉ 22 rue Meynadier, Cannes ☎ 04 93 39 63 68 🚊 Cannes

### JACQUES LOUP

www.jacques-loup.com
This family-run luxury shoe shop carries all the top names, as well as brands you might not find in other shops.
🞥 Off map to west ✉ 21 and 47 rue d'Antibes, Cannes ☎ 04 93 39 28 35
🚆 Cannes

### LALIQUE

Its very name conjures up belle-époque style and elegance. A century on, its range has expanded beyond crystal and glass to include jewellery, leather goods, decorative items and perfumes.
🞥 Off map to west ✉ 87 rue d'Antibes, Cannes ☎ 04 93 38 66 88 🚆 Cannes

### LENÔTRE

Cannes is the only place outside Paris with this luxury delicatessen, which also has a café and cooking workshops.
🞥 Off map to west ✉ 63 rue d'Antibes, Cannes ☎ 04 97 06 67 67 🚆 Cannes

## Grasse
### ETS VALLAURI

A great range of local products, from fine wines to olive oils and confectionary, are sold here.
🞥 Off map to west ✉ 2 rue Dominique Conte, Grasse ☎ 04 93 36 59 25 🚌 500

### FRAGONARD

www.fragonard.com
Part of the famous Fragonard perfumery, this shop has a wonderful

stock of perfumes, soaps and gift items, as well as running two-hour courses on perfumes in either French or English. There are tours here and at the factory on route de Cannes.
🞥 Off map to west ✉ 20 boulevard Fragonard, Grasse ☎ 04 93 36 44 65 🚌 500

### GALIMARD

www.galimard.com
At this shop you can take factory tours and even blend your own perfume.
🞥 Off map to west ✉ 73 route de Cannes, Grasse ☎ 04 93 09 20 00 🚌 500

### LILÔ CHAPÔ

www.creationsfrancoise-b.com
Milliner Françoise Boyat makes delightful women's hats in many styles, shades and fabrics, and will create a hat to order. She also sells men's hats.
🞥 Off map to west ✉ 9 rue Jean Ossola, Grasse ☎ 04 93 42 73 21 🚌 500

---

#### AFFORDABLE CANNES

Although La Croisette is lined with the likes of Dior, Lacroix, Chanel, Ferragamo and Dolce & Gabbana, Cannes has shopping for every budget. Rue d'Antibes, just behind La Croisette, has middle-range shops, the FNAC department store and more affordable designers like Tara Jarmon. Pedestrian rue Meynadier has budget chains and souvenir shops.

---

### MOLINARD

www.molinard.com
Molinard has tours and courses and a chance to buy at factory prices.
🞥 Off map to west ✉ 60 boulevard Victor Hugo, Grasse ☎ 04 92 42 33 11 🚌 500

## St-Paul-de-Vence
### GALERIE LE CAPRICORNE

www.galecapricorne.com
These two galleries are among the oldest in the village and specialize in paintings and sculptures by leading artists. No. 64 has master engravings by Chagall, Picasso and Miró.
🞥 Off map to west ✉ 15 and 64 rue Grande, St-Paul ☎ 04 93 58 34 42 🚌 400

### SAINT-PAUL IMAGES

For the picture-perfect memory of this beautiful hilltop village, this shop sells old photos, posters, postcards and paintings by Provençal artists.
🞥 Off map to west ✉ 3 Montée de l'Eglise, St-Paul ☎ 04 93 24 37 48 🚌 400

## Vallauris
### GALERIE MADOURA

This is the workshop where Picasso discovered ceramic art, and it still has the rights to reproduce some of his designs. Limited editions are made using his original moulds.
🞥 Off map to west ✉ Off avenue Georges Clemenceau, Vallauris ☎ 04 93 64 66 39
🚆 Golfe Juan, then bus 20 to place de la Libération

## Antibes

### ABSINTHE BAR LA BALADE

Below and part of the Balade du Provence shop in the market, but with a separate entrance round the corner when the shop is closed, this vaulted cavernous bar offers more than 30 different kinds of absinthe, as well as other drinks.

➕ Off map west along coast ✉ 25 Cours Masséna, Antibes ☎ 04 93 34 93 00 🕐 Daily 9am–10pm 🚉 Antibes

### ANTIBES BOWLING

www.cannesbowling.com/antibes

As well as 22 ten-pin bowling lanes, this venue has an English-style pub, restaurant, bar and 21 pool tables.

➕ Off map west along coast ✉ 275 Première Avenue, Antibes ☎ 04 92 91 70 30 🕐 Daily 2pm–2.30am (4am on weekends) 🚉 Antibes

## Cagnes-sur-Mer

### CASINO DE CAGNES-SUR-MER

www.groupetranchant.com

This small casino has 30 slot machines, dinner and party events every Friday and Saturday evening and a gaming room with English roulette, blackjack and other games.

➕ Off map west along coast ✉ 116 boulevard de la Plage, Cagnes-sur-Mer ☎ 04 92 27 14 40 🕐 Daily 10am–4am 🚉 Cagnes-sur-Mer

### CINEMA ESPACE CENTRE

www.cagnes-tourisme.com

This 336-seat cinema is right in the heart of town and shows inexpensive previews of new movies as well as recent releases. On the third Thursday of each month their Cinema Club shows films in their original language, with French subtitles, followed by a discussion.

➕ Off map west along coast ✉ 5 avenue de Verdun, Cagnes-sur-Mer ☎ 08 92 68 01 26 (€0.31/min) 🚉 Cagnes-sur-Mer

### HIPPODROME DE LA CÔTE D'AZUR

www.hippodrome-cotedazur.com

There are horse races at this stadium by the sea two or three days a week in summer. Other events include motorbike racing and food exhibitions.

➕ Off map west along coast ✉ Avenue de Cannes, Cagnes-sur-Mer ☎ 04 93 22 51 00 🚉 Cagnes-sur-Mer

### CANNES FILM FESTIVAL

The Cannes Film Festival began in 1939 as the French reaction to what they saw as the increasingly fascist films being selected for the Venice Film Festival. It is now such an established event that it has become a film star itself, featuring in several movies, such as *Mr Bean's Holiday*, starring Rowan Atkinson.

## Cannes

### AU BUREAU

www.aubureau-cannes.com

This great nightspot, a combination restaurant, lounge bar and pub, starts early with a 6–8pm 'happy hour' and tapas, before the DJ moves in with dance music. It's one block back from the north side of the port.

➕ Off map west along coast ✉ 49 rue Félix-Faure, Cannes ☎ 04 93 68 56 36 🕐 Daily 6pm–late 🚉 Cannes

### CANNES BOWLING

www.cannesbowling.com

Extremely popular late-night hang-out, with 16 ten-pin bowling lanes, 21 pool tables, an American bar, an English-style pub and a restaurant.

➕ Off map west along coast ✉ 189 boulevard Francis Tonner, Cannes La Bocca ☎ 04 93 47 02 25 🕐 Daily 3pm–4am 🚉 Cannes

### CASINO BARRIÈRE DE CANNES

www.casino-barriere-lesprinces.com

Here you'll find roulette tables, blackjack, stud poker and *punto banco* games; also slot machines offering pay-outs of up to €200,000. Les Princes cocktail bar is a fashionable drinking spot.

➕ Off map west along coast ✉ 50 boulevard de la Croisette, Cannes ☎ 04 97 06 18 50 🕐 Daily 8pm–4am (tables), 1pm–4am (slots); until 5am in summer 🚉 Cannes

## FIREWORKS SHOWS

www.festival-pyrotechnique-cannes.com
Every summer Cannes has a Fireworks Festival, or *Festival d'Art Pyrotechnique*, with spectacular displays put on about once a week out in the bay in which firework artists from all over the world are invited to show what they can do.
⊞ Off map west along coast
✉ Baie de Cannes ☎ 04 92 99 33 83 🕓 Jul, Aug 10pm
🚊 Cannes

## PALAIS DES FESTIVALS

www.palaisdesfestivals.com
If your ticket to the Cannes Film Festival (▷ panel, 103) failed to arrive, you can still see the venue where all the main showings take place by attending a concert at the Palais des Festivals. In summer there are concerts almost every night, from pop and rock to jazz and classical, alongside exhibitions and, of course, cinema screenings.
⊞ Off map west along coast
✉ Boulevard de la Croisette, Cannes ☎ 04 92 99 33 83
🚊 Cannes

## LES PLAGES ÉLECTRONIQUES

www.plages-electroniques.com
Most Wednesdays in July and early August the beach at the Palais des Festivals explodes with

the sounds of electronic music as it is turned into one giant outdoor club, with themed nights devoted to electro, techno, jungle drum and bass, hip-hop and other music styles.
⊞ Off map west along coast
✉ Plage du Palais des Festivals, Cannes ☎ 06 11 30 22 63 🕓 Usually Wed 7.30pm–12.30am 🚊 Cannes

## Èze
### ASTRORAMA

www.astrorama.net
In the hilly park north of Èze village is this star and space observatory. Its planetarium is open in the evenings but also puts on a special star show, the Spectacle aux Étoiles, on certain days.
⊞ Off map east along coast
✉ Route de la Revère, Èze
☎ 04 93 85 85 58
🕓 Mar–end Jun, Sep–end Dec Fri, Sat 6–10.30pm; Jul, Aug Mon–Sat 6–10.30pm
🚫 No public transport

---

### ALL THAT JAZZ

France has always loved jazz, and jazz musicians love France, particularly Paris, where many jazz musicians from the US have settled over the years. But there is a mutual admiration society on the Côte d'Azur, too. In addition to the big Nice Jazz Festival (▷ 114), there is the annual Antibes Juan-les-Pins Jazz Festival, going strong since 1960.

---

## Monaco
### LES BALLETS DE MONTE-CARLO

www.balletsdemontecarlo.com
Launched in 1985 by Princess Caroline, carrying out the wishes of her mother Princess Grace, the Monte-Carlo Ballet stages classical and contemporary dance.
⊞ Off map east along coast
✉ Grimaldi Forum, 10 avenue Princesse Grace, Monaco
☎ 377 98 06 28 56
🚊 Monaco-Monte-Carlo

### CASINO DE MONTE-CARLO

See page 92.

### OPÉRA DE MONTE-CARLO

www.opera.mc
The 524-seat Salle Garnier opened in 1879, designed by Charles Garnier. With only a short season and such an intimate theatre, tickets can be hard to get, but it is certainly worth trying.
⊞ Off map east along coast
✉ 10 avenue Princesse Grace, Monaco ☎ 377 92 16 22 99
🕓 Jan–end Mar
🚊 Monaco-Monte-Carlo

### SPORTING MONTE-CARLO

www.sportingmontecarlo.com
The Sporting Club has bars, a casino, Jimmy'z club and Bar Boeuf et Co restaurant (▷ 106).
⊞ Off map east along coast
✉ Avenue Princesse Grace, Monaco ☎ 377 98 06 36 36
🚊 Monaco-Monte-Carlo

# Restaurants

## Antibes

### BACON (€€€)

www.restaurantdebacon.com
It began in 1948 as two trestle tables, and by 1985 the Bacon had earned its first Michelin star, which it still has today. Panoramic views and the best fresh fish dishes are key attractions.
➕ Off map to west
✉ Boulevard de Bacon, Cap d'Antibes, Antibes ☎ 04 93 61 50 02 🕐 Feb–end Oct Tue dinner, Wed–Sun lunch, dinner
🚉 Antibes

## Beaulieu-sur-Mer

### LES AGAVES (€€)

Enjoy superb local cuisine in this much-lauded wood-panelled restaurant.
➕ Off map to east
✉ 4 avenue Maréchal Foch, Beaulieu-sur-Mer ☎ 04 93 01 13 12 🕐 Daily dinner only
🚉 Beaulieu-sur-Mer

## Cagnes-sur-Mer

### FLEUR DE SEL (€€)

Sample simple but delicious Provençal food in a 200-year-old house next to the church.
➕ Off map to west ✉ 85 Montée de la Bourgade, Haut-de-Cagnes ☎ 04 93 20 33 33
🕐 Fri–Tue lunch, dinner, Thu dinner 🚉 Cagnes-sur-Mer

### JOSY-JO (€€)

www.restaurant-josyjo.com
In what was once the home and studio of Modigliani, this simple, no-frills place offers friendly service and superior Provençal dishes. The grills are especially good, as are the seasonal dishes.
➕ Off map to west ✉ 8 place du Planastel, Haut-de-Cagnes ☎ 04 93 20 68 76
🕐 Mon–Fri lunch, dinner, Sat dinner; closed mid-Nov to mid-Dec 🚉 Cagnes-sur-Mer

## Cannes

### LE CAVEAU 30 (€€)

www.lecaveau30.com
Seafood is the focus at this 1930s-style brasserie, but there's a good choice of meats, too. Choose from the restaurant menu or the less expensive bistro menu.
➕ Off map to west ✉ 45 avenue Félix Faure, Cannes ☎ 04 93 39 06 33 🕐 Daily lunch, dinner 🚉 Cannes

### NICER THAN NICE'S?

In Cannes they have their own version of the Nice dish, *socca*. *Panisses* are made from the same combination of chickpea flour, olive oil and water, mixed into a dough, but instead of being oven-baked the dough is cut into squares, or into strips like French fries, and fried in a pan. If you want to try them at home you can buy the dough ready-made in Cannes' Forville market.

### CÔTÉ JARDIN (€€)

Away from the touristy glitz of La Croisette, the Côté Jardin is where locals who care about food go for a meal out. Get a table in the garden and sample the restaurant's modern take on traditional Provençal food.
➕ Off map to west ✉ 12 avenue St-Louis, Cannes ☎ 04 93 38 60 28
🕐 Tue–Sat lunch, dinner
🚉 Cannes

### LE FESTIVAL (€€€)

www.lefestival.fr
The place to see and be seen during the Film Festival, with a great view and a choice of the restaurant or the more relaxed Grill Room. Dishes range from lobster bouillabaisse to salads and daily specials.
➕ Off map to west ✉ 52 La Croisette, Cannes ☎ 04 93 38 04 81 🕐 Daily 9am–11pm (until midnight Jul, Aug and during Cannes Film Festival)
🚉 Cannes

### LA PALME D'OR (€€€)

www.hotel-martinez.com
With movie star portraits on the walls, an art deco interior, views over La Croisette and two Michelin stars for its food, the Palme d'Or has it all.
➕ Off map to west ✉ Hôtel Martinez, 73 La Croisette, Cannes ☎ 04 92 98 74 14
🕐 Tue–Sat lunch, dinner; closed Nov to mid-Dec
🚉 Cannes

## Èze

### CHÂTEAU DE LA CHÈVRE D'OR (€€€)

www.chevredor.com
Clinging to the rocky side of the stunning village of Èze, this restaurant has two Michelin stars and one of the most romantic settings on the coast.
✠ Off map to east
✉ Moyenne Corniche, rue du Barri, Èze ☎ 04 92 10 66 66 ☼ March–end Oct daily lunch, dinner; closed Wed in Mar ▦ 82

## Grasse

### CAFÉ DES MUSÉES (€–€€)

This café is owned by the Fragonard Perfume Factory, in the heart of Grasse. It has indulgent pastries and beautifully prepared salads.
✠ Off map to west ✉ 1 rue Ossola, Grasse ☎ 04 92 60 99 00 ☼ Mon–Fri 8.30–6.30, Sat, Sun 9–6 ▦ 500

## Monaco

### BAR BOEUF ET CO (€€€)

www.alain-ducasse.com
Alain Ducasse's more casual Monaco restaurant, overlooking the sea, began by focusing on sea bass (bar) and beef but the menu has now expanded. Simple-sounding dishes become mouth-watering treats.
✠ Off map to east
✉ Sporting Monte-Carlo, avenue Princesse Grace, Monaco ☎ 377 98 06 71 71 ☼ May–Sep daily dinner only ▤ Monaco-Monte-Carlo

### LE CAFÉ DE PARIS (€€)

This is a perfect place for people-watching by Monte-Carlo's casino, sipping a coffee or a glass of wine or enjoying some fresh fish or a less expensive plat du jour.
✠ Off map to east ✉ Place du Casino, Monaco ☎ 377 92 16 20 20 ☼ Daily 7am–1am ▤ Monaco-Monte-Carlo

### LE LOUIS XV (€€€)

www.alain-ducasse.com
One of the best eating experiences around is the flagship restaurant from Alain Ducasse, with its three Michelin stars. The service is impeccable yet friendly.
✠ Off map to east ✉ Hôtel de Paris, place du Casino, Monaco ☎ 377 98 06 88 64 ☼ Thu–Mon lunch, dinner, and Wed dinner mid-Jun to mid-Aug; closed late-Nov to late-Dec ▤ Monaco-Monte-Carlo

---

### THE MICHELIN STAR

In France the Michelin star is the ultimate accolade for a restaurant. The top rating of three stars guarantees the meal of a lifetime, and at the time of writing only 26 restaurants in the whole of France have this honour—and ten of those are in Paris. In the area covered by this book there is only one three-star restaurant, Alain Ducasse's Le Louis XV in Monaco (▷ this page).

---

## St-Paul-de-Vence

### LA COLOMBE D'OR (€€)

www.la-colombe-dor.com
This famous restaurant has been patronized by artists and stars from Picasso to Elton John. Poached sea bass is one special, although all the food is special.
✠ Off map to west ✉ 1 place du Général-de-Gaulle, St-Paul-de-Vence ☎ 04 93 32 80 02 ☼ Daily lunch, dinner; closed Nov, Dec and some days in Jan ▦ 400

### LE SAINT PAUL (€€€)

www.lesaintpaul.com
This Michelin-starred restaurant serves top-notch Provençal cooking for a romantic evening or an indulgent lunch.
✠ Off map to west ✉ 86 rue Grande, St-Paul-de-Vence ☎ 04 93 32 65 25 ☼ Daily lunch, dinner; closed Tue, Wed Nov–end March, Tue–Thu lunch in Apr and Oct ▦ 400

## Villefranche-sur-Mer

### LA MÈRE GERMAINE (€€€)

www.meregermaine.com
The eponymous Mère Germaine founded this restaurant in 1938. The bouillabaisse is said to be one of the best this side of Marseille.
✠ Off map to east ✉ 9 quai Courbet, Villefranche-sur-Mer ☎ 04 93 01 71 39 ☼ Daily lunch, dinner; closed mid-Nov to Christmas ▤ Villefranche-sur-Mer

Whether you prefer small family-owned hotels, modern chains, holiday apartments or luxury hotels that recall the era of the belle époque, Nice has a good range of accommodation to suit every budget.

Where to Stay

# Introduction

With nearly 200 hotels and 10,000 rooms, Nice ranks second in France for accommodation. An upgrading of facilities in the past decade has added modern design, technology, comfort and services to many hotels.

### Location, Location

The south of France is more expensive than other regions of the country outside Paris. Book well ahead if you're looking for a bargain. The cheapest hotels in Nice are near the station, a relatively safe, if somewhat down-at-the-heel, area. Mid-range hotels are largely found along the central avenues and boulevards. There are few hotels in the Vieille Ville. Luxury hotels occupy the prime position along the central stretch of the Promenade des Anglais and its side streets. Those travelling by car may find parking easier in motels near the airport.

### Book Ahead

Nice may have a wealth of hotel rooms, but they can fill up quickly, especially in summer. There is an influx of foreign tourists from June onwards, and in late July and August the French head for the coast for their summer holidays. Nice is a leading convention city, and events elsewhere on the Côte d'Azur, such as Monaco's Grand Prix, can also affect hotel availability. The Nice Convention and Visitors Bureau operates a free hotel reservation system. Book online at www.niceres.com or by phone on +33 (0) 892 707 407 (€0.34 per minute). For last-minute reservations, try a tourist information office.

## HOTEL RATINGS

Hotel classifications range from 'No Stars' to '4-Star Luxe', depending on the standard of the amenities and general upkeep. The ratings can be misleading, though, as some hotels with lower ratings are lovely. Rooms often vary widely within a hotel, so ask to see a room before checking in and request another if it's not suitable. Prices are normally quoted per room, rather than per person. There is an additional charge for breakfast, from €6, so you may prefer to find a *boulangerie* or outdoor café.

## PRICES

Expect to pay under €85 per night for a double room in a budget hotel.

## HÔTEL ARMENONVILLE

www.hotel-armenonville.com
With only 12 rooms, a car park, a reasonably central location, free wireless internet access and a lovely little garden, the Armenonville is great if you don't mind simple but pleasant rooms.

➕ D7 ✉ 20 avenue des Fleurs ☎ 04 93 96 86 00; fax 04 93 44 66 53 🚌 38

## HÔTEL DU CENTRE

www.nice-hotel-centre.com
A five-minute walk from the train station, the Hôtel du Centre has 26 rooms, ranging from basic ones at the back to pleasant front-facing rooms, some decorated in the styles of artists associated with the south of France. The cheapest rooms are not ensuite, but the staff are very friendly and there's free WiFi in the lobby and the restaurant next door.

➕ F6 ✉ 2 rue de Suisse ☎ 04 93 88 83 85; fax 04 93 82 29 80 🚌 23, 99 🚉 Gare SNCF

## HÔTEL DANEMARK

www.hotel-danemark.com
The Danemark is in a residential district west of the city centre but only a short stroll to the Promenade des Anglais. It has 12 rooms, simple but quite stylish for the price, and there's a terrace for breakfast and relaxing.

➕ D7 ✉ 3 avenue des Baumettes ☎ 04 93 44 12 04; fax 04 93 44 56 75 🚌 38

## HÔTEL DURANTE

www.hotel-durante.com
The Hôtel Durante is a decent 3-star option in a lively neighbourhood just south of the train station. It's convenient for many of Nice's sights, but a bit of a walk to the old town. There are 24 rooms, simple but clean, and a hidden garden, too.

➕ F6 ✉ 16 avenue Durante ☎ 04 93 88 84 40; fax 04 93 87 77 76 🚉 Gare SNCF

## HÔTEL FÉLIX BEACH

www.hotel-felix.com
The 2-star Félix is in an ideal location on a pedestrian street close to the Place Masséna, with shops and restaurants

## YOUTH HOSTELS

Nice has several youth hostels, known as *auberges de jeunesse*. You normally need to be a student or member of the International Youth Hostel Association (IYHA) to stay in one. Nice Camélias hostel, at 3 rue Spitaliéri (☎ 04 93 62 15 54, www.hihostels.com) is in the town centre, near the train station. Nice Mont Boron is east of the town centre, on route Forestière du Mont Alban (☎ 04 93 89 23 64, www.hihostels.com).

right outside the door and the Promenade des Anglais just a short stroll away. With only 14 rooms, starting as low as €55 per night, it books up well ahead.

➕ F7 ✉ 41 rue Masséna ☎ 04 93 88 67 73; fax 04 93 16 15 78 🚌 15

## HÔTEL VILLA LA TOUR

www.villa-la-tour.com
Some of the rooms in this old-town hotel are small and there's no lift, but what the hotel lacks in grandeur it more than makes up for in charm, friendliness and convenience—it's a short walk from the bus station. The 16 rooms range from simple singles to larger rooms with views over the old town. There's also a tiny roof garden.

➕ H6 ✉ 4 rue de la Tour ☎ 04 93 80 08 15; fax 04 93 85 10 58 🚌 All buses to the Gare Routière

## HÔTEL WINDSOR

www.hotelwindsornice.com
This hotel is a few blocks back from the Negresco, and like the Negresco it will appeal to art-lovers. Each of its 57 rooms has been given over to an artist to decorate, or has been decorated with posters or frescoes. The website shows the various styles. There is a pool, health club and sauna.

➕ F7 ✉ 11 rue Dalpozzo ☎ 04 93 88 59 35; fax 04 93 88 94 57 🚌 9, 10, 22

# Mid-Range Hotels

## BOSCOLO PARK HÔTEL

www.boscolohotels.com

The Park, part of the Boscolo group, is an affordable yet smart option very close to Place Masséna and the Jardin Albert I. Some of the 104 rooms and 4 suites overlook the gardens, and the decor is in classical style, using Provençal furniture. There is no restaurant, but there are dozens of good eating options in the surrounding streets.

🔒 F7 ⊠ 6 avenue Suède ☎ 04 97 03 19 00; fax 04 93 82 29 27 🚌 11, 98 and all buses on Promenade des Anglais

## HÔTEL ANIS

www.hotel-anis.com

In a residential district to the west of the city centre, the three-star Anis is not in the midst of things, but is an attractive option if you don't like staying in the heart of the action. There are gardens with olive and lemon trees, a pool and 42 spacious rooms, many with terraces and some with sea views.

🔒 Off map at A9 ⊠ 50 avenue de la Lanterne ☎ 04 93 18 29 00; fax 04 93 83 31 16 🚌 12, 23

## HÔTEL BEAU RIVAGE

www.nicebeaurivage.com

On the Promenade des Anglais (though the entrance is in the street behind), this grand old building was renovated in 2004. It now has 107 rooms and 11 suites, which are a mix of modern minimalist design and Provençal touches, with shutters and balconies, some looking over the Baie des Anges.

🔒 G7 ⊠ 24 rue St-François-de-Paule ☎ 04 92 47 82 82; fax 04 9 2 47 82 83 🚌 All buses to the Gare Routière

## HÔTEL GOUNOD

www.gounod-nice.com

The Gounod has a grand exterior dating from 1910, and it's an excellent affordable choice if you want to be near the city centre. There are 46 rooms and suites, and all are air-conditioned and

ensuite, with satellite TV. Guests can use the facilities, including a rooftop swimming pool and Jacuzzi, at the more expensive Hôtel Splendid (▷ 111).

🔒 E6 ⊠ 3 rue Gounod ☎ 04 93 16 42 00; fax 04 93 88 23 84 🕔 Closed from late Nov to late Dec 🚌 8

## HÔTEL HI

www.hi-hotel.net

Guests either love or hate the Hi, with its 38 rooms each designed to one of nine different concepts, from blinding white to bright green. It's no surprise to find that one of the design team worked with Philippe Starck. What the hotel does, it does well, but you have to be sure it's for you.

🔒 E7 ⊠ 3 avenue des Fleurs ☎ 04 97 07 26 26; fax 04 97 07 26 27 🚌 23

## HÔTEL DE MADRID

www.hotelmadridnice.com

Part of the Best Western chain, this pleasant three-star hotel is less than a five-minute walk from the train station. On the corner with avenue Jean Médecin, it's also a quick tram or bus ride to the Promenade des Anglais. The 44 bedrooms are smartly decorated and all have air-conditioning, satellite TV and WiFi access. Some have balconies overlooking the pedestrian street, while superior rooms also have living room areas.

✚ F5 ✉ 3 rue de Belgique
☎ 04 93 88 85 18, fax 04 93
88 55 27 🚉 Gare SNCF

## HÔTEL MASSÉNA

www.hotel-massena-nice.com
This four-star hotel is in
an ideal location, not far
from anywhere—the
beach, the old town, the
museums. It has 110
rooms in a variety of
styles, from subdued
modern to Provençal. All
are air-conditioned and
sound-proofed, and come
with flat-screen TV and
internet connection.
There's free WiFi access
in the reception areas.
✚ G7 ✉ 58 rue Gioffredo
☎ 04 92 47 88 88; fax 04 92
47 88 89 🚌 15

## HÔTEL NAUTICA

www.hotelnautica.com
As the name suggests,
the Nautica has a nautical
theme in its public areas
and is near the port.
There are 89 modern air-
conditioned rooms, with
the standard you would
expect from a Best
Western hotel.
✚ K6 ✉ 38 rue Barbéris
☎ 04 92 00 21 21; fax 04 92
00 21 22 🚌 1, 2, 9 ,10

## HÔTEL NICE RIVIERA

www.hotel-nice-riviera.com
The four-star Nice Riviera
is in a good location, just
off the central avenue
Jean Médecin. It has 122
modern rooms, in bold
red and yellow hues,
some of them with
terraces. There's a car
park beneath the hotel,
which is a bonus in Nice,
and the seafront is only
a short walk away.
✚ G6 ✉ 47 rue Pastorelli
☎ 04 93 92 69 60; fax 04 93
92 69 22 🚌 4, 7, 22 and
others

## HÔTEL SPLENDID

www.splendid-nice.com
About 400m back from
the Promenade des
Anglais, on the busy but
appealing boulevard
Victor Hugo, the four-star
Splendid has been in the
same family for three
generations. It has a magnificent rooftop pool and
Jacuzzi, where you feel
hidden away from the
city. There's a sauna and
small spa, an eighth-floor
bar and dining room with
panoramic views, and
many of the 127 rooms
and suites have private
balconies or terraces.
✚ E7 ✉ 50 boulevard Victor
Hugo ☎ 04 93 16 41 00; fax
04 93 14 42 70 🚌 9, 10

## HOLIDAY APARTMENTS

A good option to consider if
you are travelling as a family
or small group and staying a
week or more is a holiday
apartment, known as a
*résidence*. Many of these are
along the Promenade des
Anglais or centrally located in
modern buildings, with
kitchens and other amenities.
They can be booked through
the tourist office (▷ 122).
They are listed online or ask
for the *Guide des Locations
de Vacances de Nice*.

## IBIS NICE CENTRE GARE

www.accor.com
This 199-room hotel, one
of the Ibis chain, is right
by the station, from
where there is also a
direct bus to the airport.
It's ideal if you plan to
take the train up and
down the coast, and it's
only a short walk into the
heart of the city. Rooms
are simple and clean, and
are air-conditioned and
have WiFi internet access.
✚ E6 ✉ 14 avenue Thiers
☎ 04 93 88 85 55; fax 04 93
88 58 00 🚉 Gare SNCF

## MERCURE NICE MARCHÉ AUX FLEURS

www.accor.com
The small 49-room
Mercure is a good mid-
range choice in a perfect
location, by the vibrant
Flower Market and on the
edge of the old town.
✚ H7 ✉ 91 quai des États-
Unis ☎ 04 93 85 74 19; fax
04 93 13 90 94 🚌 All buses
to the Gare Routière

## NOVOTEL NICE ARENAS AÉROPORT

www.accor.com
If you need to be near
the airport for an early
flight or late arrival, then
the ever-reliable Novotel
chain has this modern
3-star hotel, with 131
sound-proofed rooms
and a free airport
shuttle service.
✚ Off map ✉ 455
Promenade des Anglais ☎ 04
93 21 22 50; fax 04 93 21 63
50 🚌 Any airport bus

# Luxury Hotels

### PRICES

Expect to pay over €200 per night for a double room at a luxury hotel.

### ÉLYSÉE PALACE

www.elyseepalace.com
The Élysée Palace is a stunning Four Seasons hotel that manages to combine an unmissable futuristic exterior, right on the Promenade des Anglais, with a wonderful art deco interior. It has 128 rooms and 3 suites, and a fabulous rooftop swimming pool.

✚ D8 ✉ 59 Promenade des Anglais ☎ 04 93 97 90 90; fax 04 93 44 50 40 🚌 11, 52, 59, 60, 62, 94, 98

### HÔTEL NEGRESCO

www.hotel-negresco-nice.com
The Hôtel Negresco has become a Nice landmark in its own right (▷ 44–45) and is undoubtedly one of the world's great hotels. Inaugurated in 1913, it is decorated throughout by the quirky art works collected by the owner, the redoubtable Madame Augier. The 121 guestrooms and 24 suites are all uniquely designed, with each floor representing a different theme, from art deco to Louis XIII. Some have splendid balconies overlooking the Baie des Anges.

✚ E7 ✉ 37 Promenade des Anglais ☎ 04 93 16 64 00; fax 04 93 88 35 68 🚌 11, 52, 59, 60, 62, 94, 98

### PALAIS MAETERLINCK

www.palais-maeterlinck.com
The Maeterlinck has 3.5ha (9 acres) of lush landscaped gardens high above the sea, a few miles east of central Nice. It's the perfect place to get away from it all, and as well as its swimming pool it has a private beach, reached by a funicular. There are 40 rooms, including 13 suites and 11 duplexes, Each room is designed around a different colour, giving a restful feel, and almost all of the rooms have balconies overlooking the Mediterranean. There are no buses, so guests reach the hotel by taxi, car or helicopter.

✚ Off map at L9 ✉ 30 boulevard Maeterlinck ☎ 04 92 00 72 00; fax 04 92 04 18 10 🚌 None

### BELLE-ÉPOQUE HOTELS

Nice is famous for its beautiful belle-époque hotels, and, if your budget allows, there is no finer place to stay than one of these luxury palaces of a bygone era. Although the hotels have been renovated to modern luxury standards, they retain their stunning façades and atmospheric receptions and public areas. Some of the best addresses are along or near the Promenade des Anglais, and along boulevard Victor Hugo.

### PALAIS DE LA MÉDITERRANÉE

www.lepalaisdela
mediterranee.com
The wonderful art deco façade of the Palais de la Méditerranée is typical of Nice in its glory days, and though the original hotel burned down in a tragic fire, it has been restored as a hotel and conference centre. The historic frontage remains, right on the Promenade des Anglais, but inside is now a plush 188-room modern hotel with two swimming pools, a Turkish bath and casino.

✚ F7 ✉ 13–15 Promenade des Anglais ☎ 04 92 14 77 00; fax 04 92 14 77 14 🚌 11, 52, 59, 60, 62, 94, 98

### LA PÉROUSE

www.hotel-la-perouse.com
High on a cliff that is part of the Colline du Château, La Pérouse (which was once a prison) has 58 rooms and 4 suites. Many of the rooms have unrivalled views over the Baie des Anges and/or the old town, and there's a wonderful open-air swimming pool, too. The rooms are modern, with clean lines and white walls enhancing the Mediterranean light. There are no buses, so access is by car or taxi.

✚ H8 ✉ 11 quai Rauba-Capéu ☎ 04 93 62 34 63; fax 04 93 62 59 41 🚌 None

Use this section to familiarize yourself with travel to and within Nice and around the Côte d'Azur. The Essential Facts give you insider knowledge of the city.

Need to Know

# Planning Ahead

## When to Go

Nice has a temperate Mediterranean climate but winters can still be cold and wet, with most rain falling between October and March. August sees half of Paris descending on the Riviera for the annual vacation. May to early July and September are probably the ideal times to travel.

**TIME**

Nice is one hour ahead of London, six hours ahead of New York and nine hours ahead of Los Angeles.

### AVERAGE DAILY MAXIMUM TEMPERATURES

| JAN | FEB | MAR | APR | MAY | JUN | JUL | AUG | SEP | OCT | NOV | DEC |
|-----|-----|-----|-----|-----|-----|-----|-----|-----|-----|-----|-----|
| 13°C | 13°C | 15°C | 17°C | 20°C | 24°C | 27°C | 28°C | 25°C | 21°C | 16°C | 14°C |
| 55°F | 55°F | 59°F | 63°F | 68°F | 75°F | 81°F | 82°F | 77°F | 70°F | 61°F | 57°F |

**Spring** (April to May) is unpredictable, and the weather can range from summer-hot to wet and windy.

**Summer** (June to August) is almost invariably hot and dry, but there's a welcome sea breeze.

**Autumn** (September to November) can see summer temperatures lingering, with the chance of rain increasing from late October onwards.

**Winter** (December to March) is rarely below freezing and snow is an event for the locals, but it remains cold, especially at night, and it can be wet.

### WHAT'S ON

**January** The Monte-Carlo Rally takes place in Monaco.

**February/March** Nice Carnival is one of the biggest events on the Riviera, with floats designed around a different theme each year. The Gourd Festival, the *Cougourdon*, in Cimiez, is a big event to celebrate the gourd and commemorate the Feast of the Annunciation. Menton's *Fête du Citron*, or Lemon Festival, is a huge celebration, with street floats.

**May** The Cannes Film Festival is Cannes' biggest event, while in Monaco the Monaco Grand Prix sees the principality's streets turned into a racing-car circuit.

**June** The churches in Nice's old town host concerts as part of the Sacred Music Festival, and in-line skaters take over the Promenade des Anglais for two days for *Nice en Roller*. On 29 June, St. Peter's Day, the fishermen of Nice hold a Mass in the Gésu church and then parade through the streets to Les Ponchettes beach to burn a boat in honour of St. Peter.

**July** The Nice Jazz Festival comes to the Cimiez Arena.

**August/September** Nice's *Musicalia* is an annual celebration of international music in concert.

**October** St. Réparate's feast day on 8 October is celebrated with festivities in the old town on the nearest Sunday.

**December** The International Rowing Regatta is in Nice's Baie des Anges, while in place Rossetti there is the Living Nativity and in place Masséna the Christmas Fair.

## Nice Online

**www.nicetourism.com**
The Nice Convention and Visitors' Bureau
website, in French, English, German and Italian,
has impressively comprehensive coverage of
anything you might want to know. It includes
online accommodation booking and down-
loadable guides, including one for restaurants.

**www.guideriviera.com**
The official site of the regional tourist board
for the Riviera and the Côte d'Azur has links
to individual towns, as well as information on
golf, culture, business travel, water sports,
wildlife, trekking in the Alps, skiing, bungee
jumping and just about anything else you can
do on the Riviera.

**www.travelsavvy-nice.com**
An independent site that's quite small but
provides a basic guide to what to do in Nice.

**www.provencetourism.com**
The Provence Alpes Tourism Information (PATI)
site covers events, hotels, transport, weather
forecasts and other useful information from
tourism providers in the wider Provence region,
in French and English.

**http://mtcn.free.fr**
A fascinating website devoted to the traditional
music of Nice, with historical information and
photos and also sound files to listen to.

**www.nicecarnaval.com**
This website tells you all you need to know
about the Nice Carnival, in several languages,
although it's the wonderful collection of photos
that will really show you what to expect.

**www.cougourdon.com**
Unfortunately only in French, this site is
devoted to Nice's annual Gourd Festival, with
a history of the event and a guide to growing
gourds, among other things.

### PLANNING AHEAD

**www.sncf.fr**
The website of the French
train service SNCF gives
timetable and ticket information in several languages and
is an excellent pre-planning
guide for the Côte d'Azur,
which can be easily and inex-
pensively explored by train.

**www.fodors.com**
A complete travel-planning
site. You can research prices
and weather; book air tickets,
cars and rooms; ask ques-
tions (and get answers) from
fellow travellers; and find
links to other sites.

### INTERNET CAFÉS

**Internet Cyber**
www.cyberpoint-nice.com
⊞ G7 ✉ 10 avenue Félix
Faure ☎ 04 93 92 70 63
🕐 Mon–Sat 10am–9pm,
Sun 3pm–9pm 🖳 11 and
lots more 💾 90 cents for 15
mins, €3 for 1 hour

**E-mail Café**
⊞ H7 ✉ 8 rue St-Vincent
☎ 04 93 62 68 80
🕐 Mon–Sat 9am–7pm
🚌 All buses to Gare
Routière

**MacDonald's**
Several branches of
MacDonald's offer free wireless access. Some brasseries
also provide free WiFi.

# Getting There

## PASSPORTS/VISAS

Always check the latest entry requirements before you travel, as regulations can change at short notice.

## INSURANCE

EU nationals receive reduced-cost emergency medical treatment with the European Health Insurance Card (EHIC). Obtain one before travelling. Full health and travel insurance is still advised and is essential for all other travellers.

## AIRPORT

Nice-Côte d'Azur International Airport is the main gateway to this part of the Riviera. It is around 8km (5 miles) southwest of Nice, on the coast, with good bus and taxi services into the city.

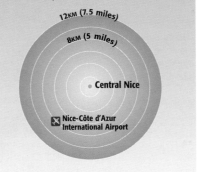

12km (7.5 miles)

8km (5 miles)

● Central Nice

✈ Nice-Côte d'Azur
International Airport

### ARRIVING BY AIR

Nice-Côte d'Azur International Airport (☎ 0820 423 333; www.nice.aeroport.fr) is the busiest airport in France outside Paris, serving around 10 million travellers a year. It is used by 54 airlines, with direct flights from 30 countries. It is also the leading airport in France for low-cost flights, serving 20 budget airlines. There are two terminals, T1 and T2, and both handle international and domestic flights, so make sure you know your terminal for the return flight. The terminals are in separate buildings, with a shuttle connection between them. There are tourist information booths in both terminals.

### AIRPORT CONNECTIONS TO THE CITY

Some airport hotels are close enough to walk to from the terminals, although finding your way out and across the main road might be tricky. For hotels farther into town, a taxi into the city should cost around €35–€40, depending on the traffic (the congestion in Nice can be heavy). The journey time is around 15–20 minutes. There are also several bus connections into the city, including a direct bus to the

main bus station (Gare Routière), although this is more expensive (€4) than catching one of the stopping services (€1.30). Buses leave from numbered stops, including Stop 5 for the city centre and Stop 4 for the train station. So check your stop and buy your tickets in advance from the ticket booth near the bus stops. There are also connecting buses for other places along the coast, including Cannes, Monte-Carlo and Cagnes-sur-Mer. There are two or three buses per hour into Nice, depending on the day and time of day, and the journey time into the city is about 30 minutes, sometimes longer if there are several stops and the traffic is bad.

### ARRIVING BY TRAIN

The Gare SNCF Nice-Ville (☎ 08 92 35 35 35) is the main station for Nice, and both TGV and local services operate from here. It is on avenue Thiers on the northern edge of the city, with bus and taxi services outside and a branch of the Tourist Information Centre to the left outside the main entrance doors. The station is close to the top of the central avenue Jean Médecin, and there are several hotels—mostly inexpensive ones—in the vicinity. It is not the smartest area of Nice, and if you are staying across town near the Promenade des Anglais or in the old town, say, then a taxi is your best option.

### ARRIVING BY BUS

The bus station for Nice, the Gare Routière (☎ 04 93 85 61 81), is at 5 boulevard Jean-Jaurès on the northwestern corner of the old town, and on the eastern side of the modern city centre. It's only a small bus station, surrounded by busy main streets, but it has very good services connecting Nice with the other towns and cities along the Côte d'Azur, as well as inland towns such as St-Paul-de-Vence and Grasse. A hotel close to either the bus or the train station is a good idea if you want to explore beyond Nice. National and international bus lines also operate from the same bus station.

# Getting Around

**IT'S ALL IN A NAME**

Several inland villages have coastal villages of the same name, but these are several kilometres away. For example, Èze is the hilltop village and Èze-sur-Mer is the resort by the sea. The coastal villages are also sometimes designated as *plage* (beach). There are different buses to each, so make sure you check the destination when boarding.

**CARTE ISABELLE**

From 1 July to 30 September there is a special train pass, the *Carte Isabelle*, which costs €12 for one day and allows unlimited travel along the Côte d'Azur. This can be useful if you plan a hectic day, but check ticket prices first as it can be cheaper to get a return to, say, Menton, and then break your journey on the way back to Nice.

## BUSES

Most bus services are operated by Ligne d'Azur (☎ 08 10 06 10 06; www.lignedazur.com), which runs the bus network within Nice and to 24 towns and villages throughout the area. The main hub is the Gare Routière bus station (☎ 04 93 85 61 81), at 5 boulevard Jean-Jaurès on the edge of the old town. There is an information booth in the station, and routes and timetables are also posted outside for checking after hours. If you're not staying near here you can get a bus route map from one of the tourist information offices or download one from the Ligne d'Azur website. There are many lines and stops on the main thoroughfares, such as the Promenade des Anglais, and most buses go to or near the Gare Routière. Timetables are available online, at the Gare Routière or at any of the Ligne d'Azur offices around Nice.

## BUS FARES

There is a simple fare structure of €1.30 per single journey, of any distance, with one change permitted within 74 minutes, but no return allowed. Pay the driver as you board, and validate your ticket in the machine. Alternatively, you can buy a one-day pass from the driver for €4, a seven-day pass for €15, a pack of 10 tickets for €10 or 20 tickets for €17. If travelling to or from the airport on the express service numbers 98 or 99, you must have a €4 pass.

## TRAINS

The Gare SNCF Nice-Ville (☎ 08 92 35 35 35) is on avenue Thiers, at the northern end of avenue Jean-Médecin. There is a very good train service along the Côte d'Azur, running east from Nice to Monte-Carlo and Menton and then on into Italy, or west through Antibes, Cannes and onwards. Some services in both directions stop at smaller stations in between, while express trains may stop only at main stations. Services are frequent and journey times much faster than by bus. Trains are only slightly more expensive than buses.

NEED TO KNOW GETTING AROUND

**118**

## TRAIN FARES

You should buy your ticket before travelling, and allow time for the queues at the ticket windows. A return ticket is often the same price as two singles. On any trip you can break the journey at any station along the way, and then resume, as long as you travel in the same direction. Remember that before you board your train you must validate your ticket at one of the machines as you go from the ticket hall towards the platforms. Failure to do so will result in an on-the-spot fine if an inspector boards the train. Even tourists are expected to know this, so excuses are not accepted. You must also re-validate your ticket if you break a journey on the way. Note that some cheap-day return tickets cannot be used on the express services at rush hour without paying a supplement, but the information boards at the stations will tell you this.

## TAXIS

Nice taxis are operated 24 hours a day by the Central Taxi Riviera company (☎ 04 93 13 78 78). There are main taxi ranks at:
- Esplanade Masséna
- Promenade des Anglais
- Place Garibaldi
- Rue Hôtel-des-Postes
- Gare SNCF
- Acropolis

## TRAM

A new tram system is currently being built in Nice. When completed, by the end of 2008, there will be several separate lines, not connecting with each other. One line, which opened in November 2007, runs from just north of Place Masséna up avenue Jean Médecin to near the train station. Another will run from Place Masséna east along boulevard Jean Jaurès to the Gare Routière and another from place Garibaldi through the Riquier district into the northeast suburbs. For more information visit www.tramway-nice.org

This open-top double decker bus is a great introduction to the city. The tour, with guided commentary, lasts about an hour and a half, and you can get on and off as often as you like at any of the 11 stops. The route includes a viewpoint over the port from Mount Boron. The bus is a good way to reach the museums of Cimiez and the Beaux-Arts museum. One- and two-day passes are available (€18 and €21).

# Essential Facts

## ELECTRICITY

French voltage is 220 volts and sockets take the Continental-type plug with two round pins. UK devices will need an adapter; US devices using 110–120 volts will need an adaptor and a transformer.

## MONEY

The official currency of France is the euro, which is also used in Monaco, even though Monaco is not a member of the European Union. Bank notes are in denominations of 5, 10, 20, 50, 100, 200 and 500 euros, and coins in denominations of 1, 2, 5, 10, 20 and 50 cents, and 1 and 2 euros.

10 euros

50 euros

200 euros

500 euros

## CREDIT CARDS

● Credit cards are widely used, with Visa and Mastercard being the most common.
● Many ATMs take credit and debit cards, and provide a choice of languages for the menus.
● Be sure to know your PIN number.

## CURRENCY EXCHANGE

● You can change foreign currency and travellers' cheques at most banks.
● The American Express bureau de change is open daily from 9am until 8pm (9pm May–Sep), 11 Promenade des Anglais ☎ 04 93 16 53 53.

## ETIQUETTE

● When meeting someone, entering a shop or a restaurant, or buying a bus or train ticket, say *bonjour* first. Foreigners who launch into a request or a demand without this opening are considered very rude. It is also considered polite to use the terms Monsieur, Madame or Mademoiselle when talking to people.
● The French language has two forms of the word 'you'. *Vous* is the common form, and *tu* is used only between close friends, or when addressing children. Never use *tu* unless the person you are speaking to uses it first.
● The French greet friends in the European manner with a kiss on the cheek, although a handshake is the correct way to greet someone until you know them better. Be guided by what the French person deems appropriate.
● Never try to get a waiter's attention by shouting *garçon*, which means 'boy'. Call the waiter *Monsieur* and the waitress *Madame*, or *Mademoiselle* if younger.

## MEDICAL TREATMENT

● Minor ailments can often be dealt with by pharmacists, who are highly trained.
● Pharmacies are indicated by a green cross, are widely available and usually open from 9 or 10am to 7 or 8pm. They operate a rota system of night openings, with locations posted on the door.

• There is a 24-hour pharmacy at 7 rue Masséna in the pedestrian area ☎ 04 93 87 78 94.
• Your hotel reception can help you find a doctor, if necessary.
• Medical treatment is usually excellent in France, but can be expensive. EU citizens can receive some medical treatment with the EHIC card, but travel insurance is always advisable.
• Hôpital Saint-Roch is a central hospital with a 24-hour emergency service ✉ 5 rue Pierre Devoluy ☎ 04 92 03 33 75.

## NATIONAL HOLIDAYS

| | |
|---|---|
| **1 Jan** | New Year's Day |
| **27 Jan** | St. Dévote's Day (Monaco only) |
| **Mar/Apr** | Easter Sunday and Monday |
| **1 May** | Labour Day |
| **8 May** | Victory Day (France only) |
| **May** | Feast of the Ascension |
| **May/Jun** | Whit Sunday and Monday |
| **Jun** | Corpus Christi (Monaco only) |
| **14 Jul** | Bastille Day (France only) |
| **15 Aug** | Feast of the Assumption |
| **1 Nov** | All Saints' Day |
| **11 Nov** | Armistice Day (France only) |
| **19 Nov** | Monaco National Day (Monaco only) |
| **8 Dec** | Feast of the Immaculate Conception (Monaco only) |
| **25 Dec** | Christmas Day |

## NEWSPAPERS

Local papers include *Nice-Matin* and *La Provence*. For listings, *Semaine des Spectacles* has weekly theatre and music events, while clubs and leisure activities can be found in the free *Le Pitchoun*. *New Riviera Côte d'Azur* is a magazine in English that has good listings.

## OPENING HOURS

• Shops are generally open Mon–Sat 9.30 or 10 to 7 or 7.30, or later during summer. Many close for lunch for an hour or so between noon and 2, and some open on Sunday mornings.
• Banks are open Mon–Fri, usually from 9 to 4 or 5, and some may close for lunch between

### TELEPHONES

Most public phones use France Telecom phone cards, which you can buy at a post office or a *tabac*.
• To call Nice from the UK dial 00 33 and then omit the zero from the 04 Nice code.
• To call the UK from Nice dial 00 44 and then omit the first zero from the local code.
• To call Nice from the US dial 011 33 and leave out the zero from the Nice 04 code.
• To call the US from Nice dial 00 1 followed by the local code then the number.
• To call Monaco from Nice, use the Monaco code of 377.

### EMERGENCY PHONE NUMBERS

• **112** General emergency number
• **15** Ambulance
• **17** Police
• **18** Fire
If you are calling from a phone box, you don't need a phone card.

## TOURIST OFFICES

✉ 5 Promenade des Anglais
☎ 08 92 70 74 07
🕐 Jun–end Sep Mon–Sat
8–8, Sun 9–6; Oct–end May
Mon–Sat 9–6

✉ Terminal 1 and 2, Nice
Airport ☎ 08 92 70 74 07
🕐 Jun–end Sep daily
8am–9pm; Oct–end May
Mon–Sat 8am–9pm

✉ Outside the train station,
avenue Thiers ☎ 08 92 70
74 07 🕐 Jun–end Sep
Mon–Sat 8–8, Sun 9–7;
Oct–end May Mon–Sat 8–7,
Sun 10–5

## CONSULATES

**British Consulate**
✉ 24 avenue de Prado,
Marseille
☎ 04 91 15 72 10
**Irish Consulate**
✉ Les Chênes Verts, 152
boulevard J. F. Kennedy,
Antibes
☎ 04 93 61 50 63
**US Consulate**
✉ 7 avenue Gustave V, Nice
☎ 04 93 88 89 55
**Canadian Consulate**
✉ 10 rue Lamartine, Nice
☎ 04 93 92 93 22
**Australian Embassy**
✉ 4 rue Jean-Rey, Paris
☎ 01 40 59 33 00
**New Zealand Embassy**
✉ 7ter rue Léonard-de-
Vince, Paris
☎ 01 45 01 43 43

12.30 and 2. Some are open on Saturday.
● Post offices generally open Mon–Fri 8 to 7
and Sat 8 to noon.

## PLACES OF WORSHIP

**Anglican** Église Anglicane de Nice ✉ 11 rue de
la Buffa ☎ 04 93 87 19 83
**Catholic** Cathédrale Sainte-Réparate
✉ Place Rossetti
**Jewish** Grande Synagogue ✉ 7 rue Gustave
Deloye ☎ 04 93 92 11 38
**Russian Orthodox** Cathédrale Orthodoxe
Russe ✉ Avenue Nicolas II ☎ 04 93 96 88 02
**Protestant** Église Réformée ✉ 21 boulevard
Victor Hugo ☎ 04 93 82 15 76
Église Luthérienne ✉ 4 rue Melchior de Vogüé
☎ 04 93 88 28 75

## POST

● You can buy stamps in post offices, tobac-
conists (*tabac*), some hotels and from some
shops that sell postcards.
● Look for yellow mailboxes to post your mail.
● Nice's main Post Office is at 21–23 avenue
Thiers (☎ 04 93 82 65 00), opposite the train
station, and is open Mon–Fri 8–7, Sat 8–noon.

## SENSIBLE PRECAUTIONS

● Nice is generally a safe city these days, and
it's surprising to learn that the narrow streets of
the old town were considered a no-go area by
locals not so long ago. Today you are unlikely
to experience any problems, although you
should beware of pickpockets in crowded areas
such as the flower market or the station. The
streets around the station are a little down-at-
heel, and you perhaps shouldn't walk around
alone very late at night.
● If you lose anything or have it stolen, you
must report the theft to a police station if you
wish to make an insurance claim.

## TOILETS

● Public toilets are fairy common and usually
clean—many are the self-cleaning type.

# Language

| BASIC VOCABULARY | |
|---|---|
| oui/ non | yes/no |
| s'il vous plaît | please |
| merci | thank you |
| excusez-moi | excuse me |
| bonjour | hello |
| bonsoir | good evening |
| au revoir | goodbye |
| parlez-vous anglais? | do you speak English? |
| je ne comprends pas | I don't understand |
| combien? | how much? |
| où est/sont…? | where is/are…? |
| ici/là | here/there |
| tournez à gauche/droite | turn left/right |
| tout droit | straight on |
| quand? | when? |
| aujourd'hui | today |
| hier | yesterday |
| demain | tomorrow |
| combien de temps? | how long? |
| à quelle heure? | at what time? |
| à quelle heure ouvrez/fermez-vous? | what time do you open/close? |
| avez-vous…? | do you have…? |
| une chambre simple | a single room |
| une chambre double | a double room |
| avec/sans salle de bains | with/without bathroom |
| le petit déjeuner | breakfast |
| le déjeuner | lunch |
| le dîner | dinner |
| c'est combien? | how much is this? |
| acceptez-vous des cartes de credit? | do you take credit cards? |
| j'ai besoin d'un médecin/dentiste | I need a doctor/dentist |
| pouvez-vous m'aider? | can you help me? |
| où est l'hôpital? | where is the hospital? |
| où est le commissariat? | where is the police station? |

| NUMBERS | |
|---|---|
| un | 1 |
| deux | 2 |
| trois | 3 |
| quatre | 4 |
| cinq | 5 |
| six | 6 |
| sept | 7 |
| huit | 8 |
| neuf | 9 |
| dix | 10 |
| onze | 11 |
| douze | 12 |
| treize | 13 |
| quatorze | 14 |
| quinze | 15 |
| seize | 16 |
| dix-sept | 17 |
| dix-huit | 18 |
| dix-neuf | 19 |
| vingt | 20 |
| vingt-et-un | 21 |
| trente | 30 |
| quarante | 40 |
| cinquante | 50 |
| soixante | 60 |
| soixante-dix | 70 |
| quatre-vingts | 80 |
| quatre-vingt-dix | 90 |
| cent | 100 |
| mille | 1,000 |

123

# Timeline

## TRAM LINES

Nice's original horse-drawn tram system of 1880 was electrified in 1900. But it was torn out in the 1950s, giving way to the age of the automobile. In recent years, concern over pollution, congestion and global warming has led cities throughout France to build new, electric tram systems to increase public transport. Nice's new tramline, on avenue Jean Médecin, was inaugurated in November 2007, with the other branch lines opening in 2008.

*From left to right: La Turbie's Trophée des Alpes, a reminder of the Roman era; an early photo of Nice; a cannon outside Monaco's Palais Princier; a postcard of Cannes from times gone by; the Grimaldi coat of arms*

*c350BC* Nice is founded by Greeks, who first settled at Marseille. It is named Nikaïa, after Nike, the goddess of Victory.

*125BC* The Romans invade this part of what was then Gaul and call it Provincia, from where we get the name Provence.

*14BC* The Romans found their settlement of Cemenelum in what is now Cimiez. It grows to 20,000 residents and becomes the capital of the Alpes Maritimae province.

*475AD* Fall of the Roman Empire; the region becomes part of the Visigoths Empire.

*536* The Franks take over rule of the Riviera.

*600s* Nice joins the Genoese League.

*859* The Saracens pillage and burn Nice.

*1032* Provence joins the Holy Roman Empire.

*13th–14th centuries* Nice is taken over several times by the Counts of Provence.

*1388* The commune of Nice places itself under the protection of the Counts of Savoy.

*1543* Nice falls to the combined forces of King François I and Turkish privateer Barbarossa.

*1600* Nice is taken by French ducal family the House of Guise.

*1691* Nice is captured by the French military leader Nicolas Catinat.

*1696* Nice is taken back by the Counts of Savoy.

*1792* After changing between French and Spanish rule, Nice is finally taken by the armies of the First French Republic.

*1814* Nice becomes part of the kingdom of Sardinia.

*1860* The Sardinian king hands Nice to Napoleon III. Nice is once again part of France, and remains so.

*1878* Tourists start to visit the Côte d'Azur in large numbers for the mild winter climate.

*1917* Henri Matisse settles in Nice, where he remains until his death in 1954.

*1942* The Nazis invade the south of France during World War II.

*1944* Nice is liberated from the occupying German forces by the Allies.

*1962* Nice's international airport opens—by 2008 it is the second-busiest airport in France.

*1995* Jacques Peyrat becomes mayor.

*2006–08* A new tram system is created.

### GARIBALDI

Giuseppe Garibaldi was born in Nice in 1807. An Italian patriot, he fought many of the military battles that led to the unification of Italy. He tried unsuccessfully to stop his native city from being annexed to France in 1860. He died in 1882 at the age of 75. There is a statue of him in place Garibaldi, the first square to be built outside the boundaries of the medieval city in the second half of the 18th century, and renamed in his honour.

### ARTISTIC INSPIRATION

In the late 1800s and early 1900s, and again after World War II, the Côte d'Azur became a magnet for some of the greatest painters of the 20th century. They included Henri Matisse, Marc Chagall, Pierre Auguste Renoir, Pablo Picasso, Jean Cocteau and Raoul Dufy.

**NEED TO KNOW** TIMELINE

125

# Index

# CITYPACK TOP 25
# **Nice**

**WRITTEN BY** Donna Dailey
**DESIGN CONCEPT** Kate Harling
**COVER DESIGN AND DESIGN WORK** Jacqueline Bailey
**INDEXER** Marie Lorimer
**IMAGE RETOUCHING AND REPRO** Michael Moody, Sarah Montgomery
**EDITOR** Kathryn Glendenning
**SERIES EDITORS** Paul Mitchell, Edith Summerhayes

© **AUTOMOBILE ASSOCIATION DEVELOPMENTS LIMITED 2008**

First published 2008
Colour separation by Keenes, Andover
Printed and bound by Leo Paper Products, China

A CIP catalogue record for this book is available from the British Library.

**ISBN 978-0-7495-5701-0**

Published by AA Publishing, a trading name of Automobile Association Developments Limited, whose registered office is Fanum House, Basing View, Basingstoke, Hampshire RG21 4EA. Registered number 1878835.

A02959
Mapping in this title produced from map data © Tele Atlas N.V. 2007 © IGN France
Map updates courtesy of Communicarta Ltd, UK
Transport map © Communicarta Ltd, UK

The Automobile Association wishes to thank the following photographers, companies and picture libraries for their assistance in the preparation of this book.

Abbreviations for the picture credits are as follows – (t) top; (b) bottom; (c) centre; (l) left; (r) right; (AA) AA World Travel Library.

**Front cover** AA/C Sawyer; **back cover** (i) AA/J A Tims; (ii) AA/C Sawyer; (iii) Nice Convention & Visitors' Bureau; (iv) AA/J A Tims; **1** AA/J A Tims; **2/3t** AA/A Baker; **4/5t** AA/A Baker; **4tl** AA/J A Tims; **5** AA/C Sawyer; **6/7t** AA/A Baker; **6cl** AA/J A Tims; **6cr** AA/J A Tims; **6bl** AA/R Moore; **6bc** AA/C Sawyer; **6br** AA/J A Tims; **7cl** AA/J A Tims; **7cc** AA/J A Tims; **7cr** AA/J A Tims; **7bl** AA/J A Tims; **7bc** AA/J A Tims; **7br** AA/J A Tims; **8/9t** AA/A Baker; **10/11t** AA/A Baker; **10c** AA/J A Tims; **10/11c** AA/C Sawyer; **10/11b** AA/J A Tims; **11t** AA/J A Tims; **11b** AA/C Sawyer; **12/13t** AA/A Baker; **13t** AA/J A Tims; **13c** AA/C Sawyer; **13b** AA/J A Tims; **14/15t** AA/A Baker; **14tr** AA/J A Tims; **14tcr** AA/C Sawyer; **14bcr** AA/J A Tims; **14br** AA/C Sawyer; **15br** AA/J A Tims; **16/17t** AA/A Baker; **16tr** AA/J A Tims; **16cr** AA/R Moore; **16bcr** AA/J A Tims; **16b** AA/C Sawyer; **17tl** Digitalvision; **17tcl** AA/J A Tims; **17bcl** AA/C Sawyer; **17bl** AA/C Sawyer; **18t** AA/A Baker; **18tr** AA/C Sawyer; **18tcr** AA/C Sawyer; **18bcr** AA/C Sawyer; **18br** AA/J A Tims; **19t** AA/J A Tims; **19tc** AA/C Sawyer; **19c** AA/R Moore; **19bc** AA/C Sawyer; **19b** AA/A Baker; **20/21** AA/J A Tims; **24l** AA/J A Tims; **24r** AA/J A Tims; **25l** AA/J A Tims; **25r** AA/J A Tims; **26l** AA/C Sawyer; **26r** AA/J A Tims; **26/27** AA/C Sawyer; **27t** AA/J A Tims; **27bl** AA/J A Tims; **27br** AA/J A Tims; **28l** AA/J A Tims; **28r** AA/J A Tims; **29l** AA/J A Tims; **29r** AA/J A Tims; **30l** AA/J A Tims; **30r** AA/J A Tims; **30/31** AA/J A Tims; **31t** AA/J A Tims; **31bl** AA/J A Tims; **31br** AA/J A Tims; **32** AA/J A Tims; **33t** AA/J A Tims; **33bl** AA/J A Tims; **33br** AA/J A Tims; **34t** AA/J A Tims; **34bl** AA/J A Tims; **34br** AA/J A Tims; **35** AA/C Sawyer; **36/37t** AA/J A Tims; **38** AA/J Wyand; **39** AA/J A Tims; **40t** AA/J A Tims; **41** AA/J A Tims; **44l** AA/J A Tims; **44r** AA/C Sawyer; **44/45** AA/ C Sawyer; **45t** AA/R Moore; **45bl** AA/J A Tims; **45br** AA/J A Tims; **46** AA/J A Tims; **46/47** AA/J A Tims; **48l** AA/J A Tims; **48r** AA/J A Tims; **48/49** AA/J A Tims; **49l** AA/J A Tims; **49r** AA/C Sawyer; **50tl** AA/J A Tims; **50bl** AA/J A Tims; **50br** AA/J A Tims; **51t** AA/J A Tims; **52** AA/C Sawyer; **53** AA/J A Tims; **54** AA/J A Tims; **55** AA/J A Tims; **58l** AA/C Sawyer; **58c** AA/R Strange; **58r** AA/C Sawyer; **59l** AA/J A Tims; **59r** AA/J A Tims; **60l** AA/C Sawyer; **60/61** AA/R Moore; **61** AA/R Moore; **62t** AA/C Sawyer; **62bl** AA/J A Tims; **62br** AA/J A Tims; **63** AA/J A Tims; **64** AA/C Sawyer; **65** Photodisc; **66** AA/J A Tims; **67** AA/J A Tims; **68** AA/J A Tims; **69** AA/J A Tims; **72** AA/J A Tims; **72/73t** AA/J A Tims; **72/73b** AA/C Sawyer; **73bl** © Succession Henri Matisse pour les oeuvres – Photo: Ville de Nice/Musée Matisse; **73br** © Succession Henri Matisse pour les oeuvres – Photo: Ville de Nice/Musée Matisse; **74** AA/J A Tims; **74/75t** AA/J A Tims; **74/75b** AA/R Strange, Marc Chagall; © ADAGP, Paris and DACS, London 2008; **75br** AA/R Strange, Marc Chagall; © ADAGP, Paris and DACS, London 2008; **76l** AA/J A Tims; **76r** AA/J A Tims; **76/77** AA/J A Tims; **77t** AA/J A Tims; **77b** AA/J A Tims; **78t** AA/C Sawyer; **78bl** AA/J A Tims; **78br** AA/J A Tims; **79** AA/C Sawyer; **82l** AA/C Sawyer; **82tr** AA/A Baker; **82br** AA/A Baker; **83t** AA/A Baker; **83bl** AA/C Sawyer; **83br** AA/C Sawyer; **84t** AA/N Ray; **84bl** AA/C Sawyer; **84br** AA/C Sawyer; **84/85** AA/C Sawyer; **85bl** AA/C Sawyer; **85br** AA/C Sawyer; **86** AA/R Strange; **87l** AA/A Baker; **87r** AA/C Sawyer; **88l** Fondation Marguerite et Aimé Maeght, Cour Alberto Giacometti: Photo: Stéphane Briolant © Archives Fondation Maeght, Giacometti Homme qui marche II, 1960 © ADAGP, Paris and DACS, London 2008, Giacometti Femme debout I, 1960 © ADAGP, Paris and DACS, London 2008, Giacometti Homme qui marche I, 1960 © ADAGP, Paris and DACS, London 2008; **88r** AA/A Baker – Leger La Partie de campagne, 1954 © ADAGP, Paris and DACS, London 2008; **89l** AA/C Sawyer; **89r** AA/A Baker; **90l** AA/A Baker; **90tr** AA/A Baker; **90br** AA/R Strange; **91t** AA/R Strange; **91bl** AA/R Strange; **91br** AA/R Strange; **92l** AA/C Sawyer; **92r** AA/A Baker; **93** AA/C Sawyer; **94l** AA/R Strange; **94r** AA/R Moore; **95t** AA/A Baker; **95bl** AA/R Moore; **95br** © GUILLEN PHOTO-GRAPHY/ Alamy; **96/97t** AA/A Baker; **96bl** AA/A Baker; **96br** AA/N Ray; **97bl** AA/C Sawyer; **97br** AA/C Sawyer; **98/99** AA/A Baker; **98bl** AA/C Sawyer; **98br** AA/C Sawyer; **99bl** AA/R Strange; **99br** © JUPITERIMAGES/Agence Images/Alamy; **100t** AA/C Sawyer; **101** AA/J A Tims; **102** AA/J A Tims; **103** Photodisc; **104** Photodisc; **105** AA/J A Tims; **106** AA/J A Tims; **107** AA/J A Tims; **108/109t** AA/C Sawyer; **108tr** AA/C Sawyer; **108tc** AA/C Sawyer; **108bcr** AA/C Sawyer; **108br** AA/J A Tims; **110/111** AA/C Sawyer; **112** AA/C Sawyer; **113** AA/J A Tims; **114/115** AA/J A Tims; **116/117** AA/J A Tims; **116** AA/A Baker; **118/119** AA/J A Tims; **119** AA/J A Tims; **120** European Central Bank; **120/121** AA/J A Tims; **121** AA/C Sawyer; **122/123** AA/J A Tims; **124/125t** AA/J A Tims; **124bl** AA/R Strange; **124bc** AA; 124br AA/A Baker; **125bl** AA; **125br** AA/R Strange

Every effort has been made to trace the copyright holders, and we apologise in advance for any unintentional omissions or errors. We would be pleased to apply any corrections in any following edition of this publication.